crochet AT HOME

25 CLEVER PROJECTS FOR COLORFUL LIVING

edited by
BRETT BARA

INTERWEAVE
interweave.com

EDITOR **ERICA SMITH**
TECHNICAL EDITOR **JEANNIE CHIN**
ART DIRECTOR **LIZ QUAN**
DESIGNER **JULIA BOYLES**
ILLUSTRATOR **JEANNIE CHIN**
PHOTOGRAPHER **JOE HANCOCK**
STYLIST **EMILY CHOI**
PRODUCTION DESIGNER **KATHERINE JACKSON**

Interweave Press LLC
A division of F+W Media, Inc.
201 East Fourth Street
Loveland, CO 80537
interweave.com

Manufactured in China by Asia Pacific Offset Ltd.

Library of Congress
Cataloging-in-Publication Data

Bara, Brett.
  Crochet at home : 25 clever projects for
colorful living / Brett Bara.
    pages cm
  ISBN 978-1-59668-837-7 (pbk.)
  1. Crocheting--Patterns. 2. House fur-
nishings. 3. Household linens.
  I. Title.
  TT825.B2956 2013
  746.43'4--dc23

  2012048922

  10 9 8 7 6 5 4 3 2 1

contents

introduction

Nothing makes a house more like a home than filling it with your own personal touches—and what better way to do that than with crochet? Even if you don't have a ton of time to dedicate to yarn and hook, a few well-chosen handmade accessories will go a long way toward personalizing your abode.

What's more, handstitched home accents are the perfect way to freshen up your existing décor if it's gotten a little tired; they also add tons of life to basic, inexpensive pieces. Go ahead and buy that boring sofa you find on sale, because all you need are a few crocheted throw pillows or one stellar afghan to make it look like a million bucks.

When it comes to livening up your home, there's nothing more important than color. Whether you want to add a bold pop to an all-white room or are simply seeking to create an environment that's a quiet, soothing retreat, color is the secret to making it all happen. To that end, this book is all about combining clever color choices with your crocheted accents, for end results that pack a ton of punch with little effort.

If you've ever felt stumped by choosing colors for a project (and who among us hasn't?), this book is full of tips and tricks to help you navigate the world of color with ease. In no time, you'll learn to develop your own eye for color. Once you combine that with your crochet skills, you'll be an unstoppable creative force!

It was my sincere pleasure to work with some of the very best crochet designers in the industry on this book, and I think you'll love seeing many of your favorite names throughout these pages. Our team of designers created a truly inspiring collection of gorgeous projects that run the gamut from sophisticated to silly, and everything in-between. Whether you want to deck out your kitchen, bedroom, or living room, and whether you're into wild color or subdued hues—we've got it all in these pages.

So grab your hook and get ready to be inspired to transform your home with color and crochet!

Happy stitching,

brett bara

bright & modern living room

1

happy hexagons throw

SIZE
56" wide × 48" long
(142 × 122 cm).

YARN
Worsted weight (#4 Medium).

Shown here: Cascade Yarns Cascade 220 (100% Peruvian Highland wool, 220 yd [201 m]/100 g), in Brown (#2403 Chocolate), in Blues (#7816 Bluebell, #8339 Marine, #8892 Azure, #8907 Caribbean, #8908 Anis, #9427 Duck Egg Blue), in Greens (#2409 Palm, #8910 Citron, #8914 Granny Smith, #9430 Highland Green, #9566 Olive Oil), in Orange (#7824 Jack o'lantern), in Pinks (#7804 Shrimp, #9469 Hot Pink), in Purples (#7808 Purple Hyacinth, #8912 Lilac Mist, #9570 Concord Grape, #9571 Misty Lilac), in Reds (#2413 Red, #9552 Maroon, #9565 Koi), in Yellows (#2439 Gelato, #4147 Lemon Yellow, #7827 Goldenrod, #9496 Buttercup), 1 hank each.

HOOK
Size H/8 (5 mm), or size needed to obtain gauge.

NOTIONS
Tapestry needle.

GAUGE
4 rnds of hexagon patt = 4" (10 cm) in diameter. *Take time to check your gauge.*

Bold, graphic motifs in a riot of bright colors make this blanket 100 percent fun. Don't feel shy about selecting this many colors—check out our color tips in the sidebar on page 13.

DESIGNED BY MARYSE ROUDIER

STITCH GUIDE

Beg CL (beginning cluster)
(Ch 2, 1 dc) in same sp.

CL (cluster)
In next ch sp [yarn over, insert hook, yarn over and pull up loop, yarn over and draw through 2 loops] twice (3 loops on hook), yarn over, draw through all loops on hook.

Hexagon Motif

Notes

❖ Work Rnds 1 to 4 with choice colors A, B, C, and D. See instructions for working Rnd 5 and joining.

❖ When changing colors or joining a new yarn, crochet over ends to save time.

RND 1: With color A, make an adjustable ring, ch 4 (counts as 1 dc and 1 ch), [1 dc, 1 ch] 11 times, join with sl st in 3rd ch of beg t-ch, do not turn, fasten off.

RND 2: Join color B in next ch-1 sp, beg CL, ch 1, [CL, ch 1 in next ch space] 11 times, join with sl st in 2nd ch of beg t-ch, do not turn, fasten off.

RND 3: Join color C in any ch-1 sp, (beg CL, ch 3, CL, ch 1) in same sp, *(CL, ch 1) in next ch sp, (CL, ch 3, CL, ch 1) in next ch sp; rep from * 4 times more, (CL, ch 1) in last ch sp, join with sl st into 2nd ch of beg t-ch, do not turn, fasten off.

RND 4: Join color D in any ch-3 sp, (beg CL, ch 3, CL, ch 1) in same sp, *[CL, ch 1] in each of next two ch-1 sps, (CL, ch 3, CL, ch 1) in next ch-3 sp for corner; rep from * 4 times more, [CL, ch 1] in last two ch-1 sps, join with sl st in 2nd ch of beg t-ch, do not turn, fasten off.

throw

STRIP 1 (11 MOTIFS)

1st Motif

RNDS 1–4: Work Rnds 1 to 4 of hexagon motif patt with choice colors A, B, C, and D.

RND 5: Join color E in any ch-3 corner sp, (beg CL, ch 3, CL, ch 1) in same sp, *(CL, ch 1) in each of next 3 ch-1 sps, (CL, ch 3, CL, ch 1) for corner in next ch-3 sp; rep from * 4 times more, (CL, ch 1) in each of last 3 ch-1 sps, join with sl st in 2nd ch of beg t-ch, fasten off.

2nd Motif

RNDS 1–4: Work Rnds 1 to 4 of hexagon motif patt with choice colors A, B, C, and D.

ROW 5 (JOINING): Join color E in any ch-3 corner sp, (beg CL, ch 3, CL, ch 1) in same sp, *(CL, ch 1) in each of next 3 ch-1 sps, (CL, ch 3, CL, ch 1) in next ch-3 corner space; rep from * twice more, (CL, ch 1) in each of next 3 ch-1 sps, (CL, ch 1) in next ch-3 corner sp, sl st in ch-3 corner sp of previous motif, (ch 1, CL) in same ch-3 sp of current motif, [sl st in next ch-1 sp of previous motif, (CL, ch 1) in next ch-1 sp of current motif] 3 times. Sl st in next ch-1 sp of previous motif, (CL, ch 1) in ch-3 corner sp of current motif, sl st in ch-3 corner sp of previous motif, (ch 1, CL) in same ch-3 corner sp of current motif, (ch 1, CL) in each of next 3 ch-1 sps of current motif, ch 1, join with sl st in 2nd ch of beg t-ch, fasten off.

3rd to 11th Motifs

Rep as for 2nd Motif working Rnds 1 to 4 for motif and joining in Rnd 5 to previous motif.

Lay Strip 1 aside with RS facing up.

Chart Key

○ = chain (ch)

⊤ = double crochet (dc)

• = slip stitch (sl st)

⬭ = beginning cluster (beg CL)

⬭ = cluster (CL)

→ = joining

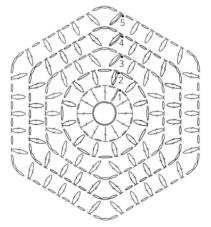

Hexagon Motif

Joining Motifs

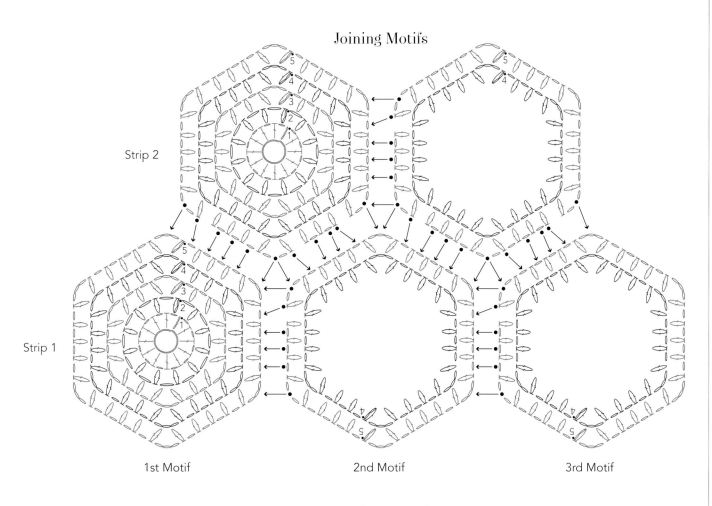

Strip 2

Strip 1

1st Motif

2nd Motif

3rd Motif

STRIP 2 (11 MOTIFS)

1st Motif

RNDS 1–4: Work Rnds 1 to 4 of hexagon patt.

RND 5 (JOINING): Join color E in any ch-3 corner sp, (beg CL, ch 3, CL, ch 1) in same sp, *(CL, ch 1) in each of next 3 ch-1 sps, (CL, ch 3, CL, ch 1) in next ch-3 corner sp, (CL, ch 1) in each of next 3 ch-1 sps, (CL, ch 1) in next ch-3 corner sp, sl st in ch-3 corner sp of 1st Motif of Strip 1, (ch 1, CL) in same ch-3 sp of current motif, [sl st in next ch-1 sp of 1st Motif of Strip 1, (CL, ch 1) in next ch-1 sp of current motif] 3 times, sl st in next ch-1 sp of 1st Motif of Strip 1, (CL, ch 1) in ch-3 corner sp of current motif, sl st in both ch-3 corner sps of 1st Motif of Strip 1 and 2nd Motif of Strip 1, (ch 1, CL) in same ch-3 corner sp of current motif, [sl st in next ch-1 sp of 2nd Motif of Strip 1, (CL, ch 1) in ch-1 sp of current motif] 3 times, sl st in next ch-1 sp of 2nd Motif of Strip 1, (CL, ch 1 in ch-3 corner sp of current motif, sl st in ch-3 sp of 2nd Motif of Strip 1, (ch 1, CL) in same ch-3 corner sp, (ch 1, CL) in each of next 3 ch-1 sps of current motif, ch 1, (CL, ch-3, CL, ch 1) in ch-3 corner sp, (ch 1, CL) in each of next 3 ch-1 sps, ch 1, join with sl st in 2nd ch of beg t-ch, fasten off.

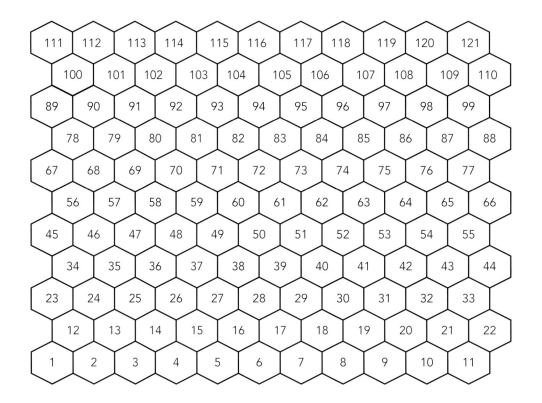

2nd Motif

RNDS 1–4: Work Rnds 1 to 4 of hexagon patt.

RND 5 (JOINING): Join color E in any ch-3 corner sp, (beg CL, ch 3, CL, ch 1) in same sp, *(CL, ch 1) in each of next 3 ch-1 sps, (CL, ch 1) in next ch-3 corner sp, sl st in ch-3 corner sp of 1st Motif of Strip 2, (ch, CL) in same ch-3 corner sp of current motif, (CL, ch 1) in each of next 3 ch-1 sps, (CL, ch 1) in next ch-3 corner sp, sl st in ch-3 corner sp of 1st Motif of Strip 1, (ch 1, CL) in same ch-3 sp of current motif, [sl st in next ch-1 sp of 1st Motif of Strip 2, (CL, ch 1) in next ch-1 sp of current motif] 3 times, sl st in next ch-1 sp of 1st Motif of Strip 2, (CL, ch 1) in ch-3 corner sp of current motif, sl st in both ch-3 corner sps of 1st Motif of Strip 2 and 2nd Motif of Strip 1, (ch 1, CL) in same ch-3 corner sp of current motif, [sl st in next ch-1 sp of 2nd Motif of Strip 1, (CL, ch 1) in ch-1 sp of current motif] 3 times, sl st in next ch-1 sp of 2nd Motif of Strip 1, (CL, ch 1) in ch-3 corner sp of current motif, sl st in both ch-3 corner sp of 2nd Motif of Strip 1 and ch-3 corner sp of 3rd Motif of Strip 1, (ch 1, CL) in same ch-3 corner sp of current motif, [sl st in next ch-1 sp of 3rd Motif of Strip 1, (ch 1, CL) in ch-1 sp of current motif] 3 times, sl st in next ch-1 sp of 3rd Motif of Strip 1, (CL, ch 1) in ch-3 corner sp of current motif, sl st in ch-3 corner sp of 3rd Motif of Strip 1, (ch 1, CL) in same ch-3 corner sp of current motif, (ch 1, CL) in each of next 3 ch-1 sps, (ch 1, CL, ch 3, CL) in next ch-3 corner sp, (ch, CL) in each of next ch-1 sp, ch 1, join with sl st in 2nd ch of beg t-ch, fasten off.

3rd to 11th Motifs
Foll diagram, rep as for 2nd Motif working Rnd 5 and joinings to Strip 1.

STRIPS 3 TO 11
Rep as for Strip 2 foll diagram, working Rnd 5 and joinings to previous completed strips.

EDGING
With RS facing, join color F in any ch-1 sp along edge.

RND 1 (RS): Ch 3 (counts as hdc and ch 1), work (1 hdc, ch 1) in each ch-1 sp, (1 hdc, ch 1) in each ch-3 sp where joined, and (3 hdc, ch 1) in each ch-3 corner sp (points) around, join with sl st in 2nd ch of beg t-ch, do not turn, fasten off.

RND 2: Join color G to any ch-1 sp, ch 1, (1 sc, ch 1) in same sp, (1 sc, ch 1) in each ch-1 sp and (3 sc, ch) in center hdc of each 3-hdc group around, join with sl st in first sc, fasten off.

FINISHING
Weave in ends.

CHOOSING COLORS

The colors in this afghan are placed randomly as you stitch; there's no specific color pattern to follow, and there's no right or wrong way to select your own hues. Here are a few tips to help you select successful shades.

- To get the same jewel effect as in this blanket, be sure to choose strong, vibrant colors. It's okay to add in a few different tones as accents, but overall keep the colors vivid rather than muted.

- In each hex, try to use a balanced mix of warm (orange, yellow, red) and cool (blue, green, purple) colors.

- It helps to have a color wheel nearby as you crochet. Complementary colors—colors that are opposite each other in the color wheel (red and green, for example)—are guaranteed to always look great together. So if you work the first round in one color, work the next round in a color that is opposite on the wheel.

- Believe it or not, adding a couple of "ugly" colors makes things interesting! So if you're working with all jewel tones, add a murky olive or a 1970s-inspired gold. It'll make those "prettier" colors pop.

- For a more cohesive and slightly less mismatched look, try using a neutral such as black, gray, white, or tan as the first or last round of every hex.

- Don't be afraid of making crazy mixes; experiment with your colors as you work and take some chances! You may find that some of your hexagons will leave you cold. You may want to trash them, but resist the urge. Once you put all of the hexes together, they'll blend into something really fabulous.

- Try to keep the blanket as a whole color balanced. In other words, avoid having your blue-dominant hexes in one corner and your reds in another.

- Have fun with it! Let yourself be free to play with the colors, and you may be surprised by the result.

ruffles & ridges pillow

SIZE

19" (48.5 cm) in diameter.

Each wedge = 9" × 2½" (23 × 6.5 cm).

YARN

Worsted weight (#4 Medium).

Shown here: Caron Vickie Howell Sheep(ish) (70% acrylic, 30% wool; 167 yd [153 m]/3 oz [85 g]), in #12 Yellow(ish) (A), #3 Grey(ish) (B), #14 Coral(ish) (C), and #5 Plum(ish) (D), 2 skeins each.

HOOK

Size I/9 (5.5 mm), or size needed to obtain gauge.

NOTIONS

19" (48.5 cm) round pillow form; tapestry needle.

GAUGE

14 ¼ sts and 13 rows = 4" (10 cm) in hdc blo. *Take time to check your gauge.*

Layers of colorful ruffles join together to create a wedged color wheel that packs a major punch in this tactile cushion. It's guaranteed to brighten up even the most boring sofa!

DESIGNED BY KATHY MERRICK

STITCH GUIDE
Blo Back loop only

Hdc2tog (Half double crochet two together)
[Yarn over, insert hook in next stitch, yarn over and pull up · loop] 2 times, yarn over and draw through all loops on hook.

pillow

BACK PANEL
Note: Work in back loops only.

1st Wedge
ROW 1 (RS): With color A, ch 33, hdc into 3rd ch from hook (ch 2 counts as first hdc throughout) and in each ch to end—32 hdc, ch 1, turn.

ROW 2: Sl st in first 8 hdc, hdc to end of row, ch 2, turn.

ROWS 3 AND 4: Hdc in next 23 hdc—24 hdc, ch 2, turn.

ROWS 5 AND 6: Hdc in next 15 hdc—16 hdc, ch 2, turn.

ROW 7: Hdc in next 7 hdc—8 hdc, ch 2, turn.

ROW 8: Hdc in next 7 hdc, fasten off color A.

2nd Wedge
Attach color B to last hdc of 1st Wedge, ch 2.

ROW 1: Hdc in next 7 hdc across in Row 8 of 1st Wedge, hdc in each of next 8-st hdc step, hdc in each of next 8-st hdc step, hdc in each of last 8-st sl st step—34 hdc, ch 1, turn.

ROWS 2-8: Rep Rows 2 to 8 of 1st Wedge, fasten off color B.

3rd and 4th Wedges
Rep as for 2nd Wedge with colors C and D.

5th to 20th Wedges
Rep as for 2nd Wedge, continuing in color sequence A, B, C, and D.

Chart Key

◡ = chain (ch)

• = slip st (sl st)

T = half double crochet (hdc)

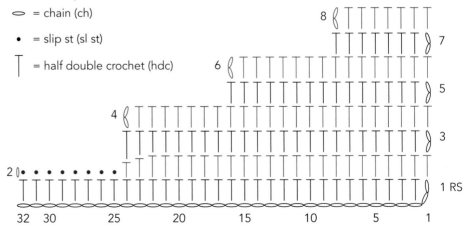

Center

Attach color A to 1st Wedge at narrow end and work around inner edge as foll:

ROW 1: Hdc in each hdc post of each wedge—20 hdc, turn.

ROWS 2 AND 3: Hdc2tog across—5 hdc, turn, do not fasten off.

Seaming

Sl st edges of 1st Wedge tog with last wedge in each st across. Fasten off.

FRONT PANEL

1st Wedge

Work Rows 1–8 as for 1st Wedge of back, do not fasten off, turn.

Ruffle

Note: Work in front loops only on RS of wedge.

ROW 1 (RS): Ch 3 (counts as first dc), *2 dc into next front loop, dc into next loop, ch 3, sc into next loop, ch 3, dc into next loop; rep from * once more, ending rep with sc in last loop, ch 10, turn.

ROW 2: Sc in first loop of next step, ch 3, dc in next loop, 2 dc in next loop, dc in next loop, ch 3, insert hook in 5th ch of ch 10 from Row 1, then sc in next loop tog with ch, ch 3, dc in next loop, 2 dc in next loop, dc in next loop, *ch 3, sc in next loop, ch 3, dc in next loop, 2 dc in next loop, dc in next loop; rep from * once more, ch 3 (does not count as dc in next row), turn.

ROW 3: *Dc into first loop, 2 dc into next loop, dc into next loop, ch 3, sc into next loop, ch 3; rep from * 4 times more, sc in last loop, ch 10, turn.

ROW 4: Rep Row 2 across 32 loops, do not ch 3, fasten off.

2nd Wedge

Work as for 2nd wedge of back, then work ruffle as for 1st Wedge of front.

3rd and 4th Wedges

Rep as for 2nd wedge with colors C and D.

5th to 20th Wedges

Rep as for 2nd wedge, continuing in color sequence A, B, C, and D.

Center and Seaming

Work as for back.

FINISHING

With WS tog, join front and back around circumference by working 8 hdc in each wedge section, leaving 4 wedges open. Do not fasten off. Insert pillow form.

Cont joining last 4 wedges of front and back tog. Fasten off. Weave in ends.

COLOR TIP

Adding one neutral (here, gray) to a colorful mix helps make projects look sophisticated rather than childlike. If gray's not your thing, try black, white, or tan.

technicolor cube ottoman

SIZE
17½" wide × 17½" long × 10½" deep (44.5 × 44.5 × 26.5 cm).

YARN
Chunky weight (#5 Bulky).

Shown here: Lion Brand Wool-Ease Chunky (80% acrylic, 20% wool; 153 yd [140 m]/5 oz [140 g]), in #630-152 Charcoal (MC), 6 skeins; in #630-133 Pumpkin (A), #630-130 Grass (B), #630-140 Deep Rose (C), #630-131 Moss (D), #630-099 Fisherman (E), and #630-146 Orchid (F), 1 skein each.

HOOK
Size K-10½ (6.5 mm), or size needed to obtain gauge.

NOTIONS
1 yd (0.91 m) of black acrylic felt; popped polystyrene beanbag refill (3.5 cubic feet); marking pins; sewing supplies; tapestry needle.

GAUGE
10 sc and 12 rows = 4" (10 cm) to make 1 panel. *Take time to check your gauge.*

Bright crocheted strips are woven together with black to create a multihued checkerboard atop this clever ottoman. Stuffed with a beanbag, this piece is sturdy enough to serve as a footstool or extra seat.

DESIGNED BY REGINA RIOUX

COLOR TIP

Simply switching the colors on this project can change its direction entirely—why not work the checkerboard in red and black, crochet some disks, and make a life-size checkers game? It's the ultimate rec room accessory!

ottoman

FRONT PANEL

(Make 8 in color MC, 2 each in colors A and B, and 1 each in colors C, D, E and F.)

Ch 43.

ROW 1: Sc in 2nd ch from hook and in each ch across—42 sc, ch 1, turn.

ROWS 2-4: Sc in each sc across, ch 1, turn.

ROW 5: Sc in each sc across, fasten off.

FRONT PANEL CONSTRUCTION

Place 8 MC color strips vertically and parallel to one another. Foll diagram, beg at top and weave first horizontal color strip laying it over one vertical strip, then under next vertical strip; cont to alternate. Secure end of first woven strip with a pin. Rep with rem color strips, alternating the start of each weave and pinning in place at outer edges.

Securing Strips

With RS facing, attach color MC through both layers at edge where pinned after corner.

RND 1: Ch 1, *40 sc evenly along first edge through both layers to secure, 3 sc in corner; rep from * twice more, 40 sc evenly along last edge, join with sl st to first sc, fasten off.

SIDE PANEL

(Make 4 in color MC.)

Ch 41.

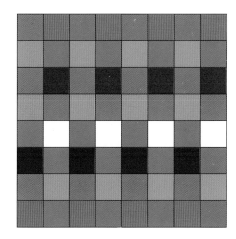

Top Panel Assembly

Color Key

- ▨ Charcoal (MC)
- ▨ Pumpkin (A)
- ▨ Grass (B)
- ▨ Deep Rose (C)
- ▨ Moss (D)
- ☐ Fisherman (E)
- ▨ Orchid (F)

ROW 1: Sc in 2nd ch from hook and in each ch across—40 sc, ch 1, turn.

ROWS 2–28: Sc in each sc across, ch 1, turn.

RND 29: *Sc in each sc across, rotate 90 degrees to right, 29 sc evenly across side to corner**, rotate 90 degrees to right; rep from * ending at **, join with sl st to beg sc, fasten off.

BACK PANEL

Ch 41 with color MC.

ROW 1: Sc in 2nd ch from hook and in each ch across—40 sc, ch 1, turn.

ROWS 2–42: Sc in each sc across, ch 1, turn.

RND 43: *Sc in each sc across, rotate 90 degrees to right, 42 sc evenly across side to corner**, rotate 90 degrees to right; rep from * ending at **, join with sl st to beg sc, fasten off.

FINISHING

Inner Cube Construction

With acrylic felt, cut 2 pieces 18" × 18" (45.5 × 45.5 cm) square and 4 pieces 18" × 11" (45.5 × 28 cm) rectangular.

Pin 4 rectangular pieces together consecutively, short side to short side, creating "box" shape. Using a ¼" (6 mm) seam allowance, sew seams.

Pin one square piece to open side of "box" and sew entire seam using a ¼" (6 mm) seam allowance. Turn box inside out.

Pin remaining square to open side of box and sew along 3 sides using a ¼" (6 mm) seam allowance.

Stuff with popped polystyrene until full and sew remaining seam.

Outer Cube Construction

Pin 4 rectangular crocheted pieces together consecutively, short side to short side, creating "box" shape (RS facing out).

ROW 1: Sl st seam tog evenly across first short side, fasten off.

Rep Row 1 for rem 3 sides.

Pin back crocheted panel to open side of "box."

RND 1: Sl st seams tog evenly around, join with sl st to first sl st, fasten off.

Turn cube over with interior of crocheted "box" facing. Place felt inner cube inside crocheted cube. Pin front crocheted panel to open side of box.

RND 2: Sl st seams tog evenly around, join with sl st to first sl st, fasten off.

Weave in ends.

switchable seasons wreaths

SIZE
14" (35.5 cm) in diameter, each wreath.

Spring Wreath
embellishments: Small Posy = 2" (5 cm) in diameter, Large Posy = 2½" (6.5 cm) in diameter.

Autumn Wreath
embellishments: Maple Leaf = 3½" (9 cm) long × 2¾" (7 cm) wide, Oak Leaf = 5" (12.5 cm) long × 3½" (9 cm) wide, Elm Leaf = 4½" (11.5 cm) long × 3¼" (8.5 cm) wide.

YARN
Autumn Wreath
Chunky weight (#5 Bulky).

Shown here: Brown Sheep Lamb's Pride Bulky (85% wool, 15% mohair; 125 yd [114 m]/4 oz [113 g]), in #83 Raspberry (A) and #81 Red Baron (B), 1 skein each.

Worsted weight (#4 Medium).

Shown here: Brown Sheep Lamb's Pride Worsted (85% wool, 15% mohair; 190 yd [173 m]/4 oz [113 g]), in #174 Wild Mustard (C), #177 Olympic Bronze (D), #280 Orange Creamsicle (E), #89 Roasted Coffee (F), and #101 Bing Cherry (G), 1 skein each.

Continued on next page
↓

Welcome the seasons in cozy style with these colorful crocheted wreaths, and change them up when the weather shifts. Simply crochet around wreath forms with bulky yarn, then pin the motifs in place, swapping them out whenever the fancy strikes.

DESIGNED BY LINDA PERMANN

YARN
Spring Wreath

Chunky weight (#5 Bulky).

Shown here: Brown Sheep Lamb's Pride Bulky (85% wool, 15% mohair; 125 yd [114 m]/4 oz [113 g]), in #11 White Frost (A), 1 skein.

Worsted weight (#4 Medium).

Shown here: Brown Sheep Lamb's Pride Worsted (85% wool, 15% mohair; 190 yd [173 m]/4 oz [113 g]), in #162 Mulberry (B), #174 Wild Mustard (C), #177 Olympic Bronze (D), #13 Sun Yellow (E), #03 Grey Heather (F), 1 skein each.

HOOK

Size J-10 (6 mm) to wrap wreath and to make embellishments with bulky yarn, or size needed to obtain measurements of embellishments.

Size 7 (4.5 mm) for embellishments with worsted weight yarn, or size needed to obtain measurements of embellishments.

Note: Use larger hook whenever using chunky weight yarn, smaller hook with worsted weight yarn.

NOTIONS

Extruded Styrofoam, 14" (35.5 cm) round, each wreath; size 21 (1⁵⁄₁₆" [10 mm] long) satin sewing pins; tapestry needle; glass pearl beads, 36 white 4mm round (for spring wreath).

GAUGE

Gauge is not critical to this project; refer to Size for measurements of each motif.

STITCH GUIDE
BPdc (back post double crochet)

Yarn over and insert hook from back to front to back around post of corresponding stitch below, yarn over and pull up a loop, [yarn over and draw through 2 loops on hook] 2 times.

Dc2tog
(double crochet two together)

[Yarn over and insert hook in stitch, yarn over and pull up a loop, yarn over and draw loop through 2 loops on hook] 2 times in same st, yarn over and draw through all 3 loops on hook.

Tr2tog
(treble crochet two together)

[Yarn over twice and insert hook in next stitch, yarn over and pull up a loop, (yarn over and draw loop through 2 loops on hook) twice] 2 times in same st, yarn over and draw through all 3 loops on hook.

Picot

Ch 3, sl st in 3rd ch from hook.

Chart Key

⬭ = ch

• = sl st

+ = sc

⊤ = hdc

† = dc

‡ = tr

= dc2tog

= tr2tog

= BPdc

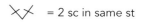 = picot

✕✕ = 2 sc in same st

autumn wreath

COVER

With color A, make slipknot leaving a 6" (15 cm) tail and place on hook.

RND 1 (WS): Join yarn A around wreath with a sc, work sc around entire wreath until completely covered making sure to work fairly tight and evenly, and ending with a multiple of 6 sts, join with sl st in first sc, turn.

EDGING

(multiple of 6 sts)

RND 2 (RS): *Skip next 2 sc, 5 dc in next sc, skip 2 sc, sl st in next st; rep from * around, ending last rep with sl in first dc, fasten off, weave in ends.

HANGING LOOP (OPTIONAL)

With color A, make slipknot leaving a 6" (15 cm) tail and place on hook. With RS of wreath facing, insert hook in any sc stitch from Rnd 1 and sl st, ch 10, reinsert hook in same st, sl st. Fasten off, drawing ends through to WS of wreath. Weave ends securely into edging stitches.

EMBELLISHMENTS

Maple Leaf

(Make 3 in color B.)

Make an adjustable ring.

RND 1 (RS): Ch 3, 11 dc in ring, join with sl st in top of beg t-ch—12 dc, do not turn.

RND 2 (RS): Ch 6, (sl st in 3rd ch from hook—picot made), dc in same sp as joining, 2 dc in each of next 2 sts, (dc, ch 5, sc in 2nd ch from hook and in next 3 chs to form stem, dc) in next st, 2 dc in each of next 2 sts, (dc, picot, dc) in next st; (sc, hdc) in next st, (dc, picot, sc) in next st, (hdc, dc, tr, picot, tr, dc, hdc) in next st, (sc, picot, dc) in next st, (hdc, sc) in last st, join with a sl st to 3rd ch of beg ch-6—5 picot points, one stem, fasten off, weave in ends.

Oak Leaf

(Make 2 in color A, 3 in color C, and 2 in color D.)

Ch 9.

RND 1 (RS): Sc in 2nd ch from hook and next 2 chs, hdc in each of next 2 chs, dc in next 2 chs, 6 dc in last ch, turn to work opposite side of foundation chain, dc in next 2 sts, hdc in next 2 sts, sc in each of remaining 3 ch, ch 1, join with sl st in first sc of rnd—6 sc, 4 hdc, 10 dc, do not turn.

RND 2 (RS): Sl st in next 2 sts, (sl st, ch 2, dc2tog, ch 2, sl st) in next st, sl st in next st, *(sc, ch 2, tr2tog, ch 2, sc) in next st*, sc in next st; rep from * to * once, sc in next st, 2 sc in next st, (ch 4, sc in 2nd ch from

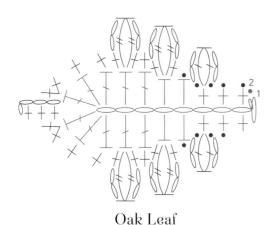

Oak Leaf

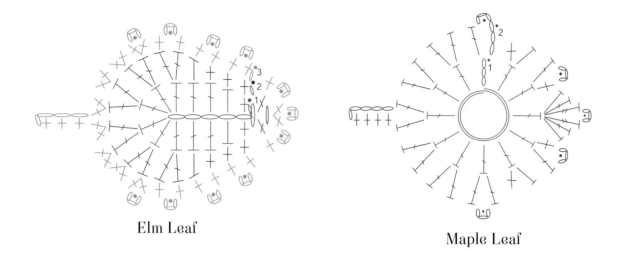

Elm Leaf

Maple Leaf

Chart Key

$\bigcirc$ = ch

$\bullet$ = sl st

$+$ = sc

$\top$ = hdc

$\dagger$ = dc

$\ddagger$ = tr

$\langle\rangle$ = dc2tog

$\langle\rangle$ = tr2tog

$\downarrow$ = BPdc

$\overline{\langle\bullet\rangle}$ = picot

$\times\!\times$ = 2 sc in same st

hook and each ch across to form stem), 2 sc in next st, sc in next 2 sts, rep from * to * once, sc in next st, rep from * to * once more, sl st in next st, (sl st, ch 2, dc2tog, ch 2, sl st) in next st, sl st in next st, fasten off—6 lobes, one stem, fasten off, weave in ends.

Elm Leaf
(Make 2 in color E.)

Ch 6.

RND 1 (RS): Sc in 2nd ch from hook, hdc in next ch, dc in next 2 chs, 6 dc in last ch, turn to work opposite side of foundation chain, dc in next 2 sts, hdc in next st, sc in remaining st, ch 1, join with sl st in first sc of rnd—2 sc, 2 hdc, 10 dc, do not turn.

RND 2 (RS): Ch 1, sc in same st as join, sc in next 2 sts, hdc in next dc, 2 dc in each of next 6 dc, hdc in next dc, sc in next 3 sts, (sc, ch 1, sc) in ch-1 sp, join with sl st in first sc—8 sc, 2 hdc. 12 dc, do not turn.

RND 3 (RS): Ch 1, (sc, picot) in same st as join, [sc in next 2 sts, picot] 3 times, sc in same st as last sc made, 2 sc in each of next 3 sts, (ch 4, sc in 2nd ch from hook and next 2 chs to form stem), 2 sc in each of next 3 sts, (sc, picot, sc) in next st, sc in next st, [picot, sc in next 2 sts] 3 times, picot, sc in ch-1 sp, picot, sc in next sc, picot, join with sl st in first sc of rnd—11 picots, 1 stem, 31 sc, fasten off, weave in ends.

Small Pointy Leaf
(Make 2 in color E.)

Rep Rnd 1 of Elm Leaf, fasten off, weave in ends.

Large Pointy Leaf
(Make 2 each in colors F and G.)

Rep Rnds 1 and 2 of Elm Leaf, fasten off, weave in ends.

FINISHING

For best results, block leaves to shape before assembling. Arrange as desired pinning leaves on wreath.

COLOR TIP

For even more versatility with this project, make more than one set of each group of motifs in different seasonal colors. The fall wreath would be perfectly summery with green leaves, and the spring wreath would be just right for the holidays in your favorite festive shades.

spring wreath

COVER

Rep as for Autumn Wreath cover with color A for Spring Wreath, ending with a multiple of 2 sts, join with sl st in first sc, turn.

EDGING
(multiple of 2 sts)

RND 1(WS): Ch 1, hdc in first sc, *sl st in next sc, hdc in next sc, rep from * around to last sc, sl st in last sc, join with sl st in first hdc, fasten off, weave in ends.

Weave in ends.

HANGING LOOP (OPTIONAL)

Rep as for Autumn Wreath with color A for Spring Wreath.

EMBELLISHMENTS

Leaf

(Make 4 in color B.)

Ch 9, rep Rnd 1 of Oak Leaf, fasten off, weave in ends.

Large Posy

(Make 2 each in colors B and C.)

Make an adjustable ring.

RND 1 (RS): Ch 3 (counts as hdc, ch 1), [hdc, ch 1] 5 times in ring, join with sl st in 2nd ch of beg t-ch—6 hdc, 6 ch-1 sps, do not turn.

RND 2 (RS): (Sl st, ch 3, 2 dc) in first ch-1 sp, 3 dc in each ch-1 sp around, join with sl st in top of beg t-ch—18 dc, do not turn.

RND 3 (RS): Ch 2 (does not count as st), [BPdc in next hdc from Rnd 1, ch 2] 6 times, join with sl st in first BPdc—6 BPdc, 6 ch-2 sps, do not turn.

RND 4: (Sl st, ch 3, 3 dc) in first ch-2 sp, 4 dc in each ch-2 sp around, join with sl st in top of beg t-ch—24 dc, do not turn.

Chart Key

⬭	= ch
•	= sl st
+	= sc
T	= hdc
ꓕ	= dc
	= tr
	= dc2tog
	= tr2tog
	= BPdc
	= picot
✕	= 2 sc in same st

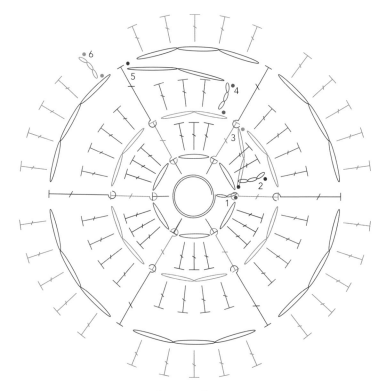

Large Posy

RND 5: Ch 2 (does not count as st), [BPdc in next BPdc from Rnd 3, ch 3] 6 times, join with sl st in first BPdc—6 BPdc, 6 ch-3 sps, do not turn.

RND 6: (Sl st, ch 3, 4 dc) in first ch-3 sp, 5 dc in each ch-3 sp around, join with sl st in top of beg t-ch—30 dc, fasten off, weave in ends.

Small Posy
(Make 2 each in colors D and E, and 3 in color F.)

Make an adjustable ring, rep Rnds 1–4 as for Large Posy, fasten off, weave in ends.

FINISHING
For best results, block embellishments to shape before assembling.

Arrange posies as desired on wreath. Thread one glass pearl onto each pin and place 3 or 4 pearled pins through the center of each flower to secure it in place. Pin leaves in place.

lace & wire bowl

SIZE
8½" (21.5 cm) in diameter ×
3½" (9 cm) high.

YARN
Shown here: Copper Wire,
(26-gauge, 200 ft/60 m), in
color Bronze, 4 spools.

HOOK
Size 4 (2 mm) steel crochet
hook, or size needed to obtain
gauge.

NOTIONS
Mill Hill glass beads, size 6,
in #16221 Bronze, 42 beads;
rolling pin; wire cutters.

GAUGE
Rnds 1–4 = 2¾" (7 cm) in
diameter. *Take time to check
your gauge.*

Try a new technique with this unique piece. Stitched in wire and adorned with beads, this bowl is a work of art in and of itself. Of course, if you don't care for bronze, try a silver tone instead!

DESIGNED BY SUSAN LOWMAN

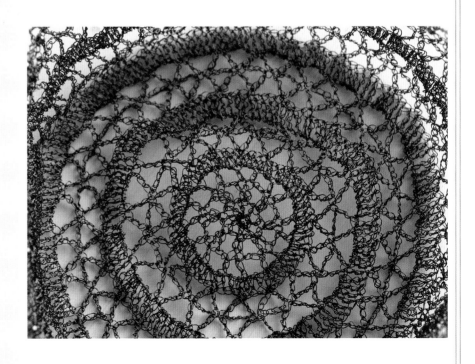

STITCH GUIDE

Bch (bead chain)
Slide a bead up to hook, yarn over and draw through loop on hook.

Bsc (bead single crochet)
Insert hook in specified st or sp and draw up a loop, slide a bead up to hook, yarn over and draw through both loops on hook.

Tr dec (treble decrease)
*Yarn over twice, insert hook in first specified st and draw up a loop, [yarn over and draw through 2 loops on hook] twice, rep from * in 2nd specified st, yarn over and draw through all 3 loops on hook.

Shell
(Tr, ch 1, tr, bch, tr, ch 1, tr) in specified st or sp.

NOTES

❖ Before starting 3rd spool of wire, thread beads onto wire and slide beads up to hook, as needed in last round to work bsc and bch. If 4th spool of wire is needed, at end of 3rd spool, remove remaining beads and thread them onto 4th spool. Continue bowl with 4th spool of wire.

❖ Periodically adjust wire stitches as wire sometimes has a mind of its own!

bowl

Ch 5, join with sl st in first ch to form a ring.

RND 1 (RS): Ch 4 (counts as dc and ch-1 sp), [dc in ring, ch 1] 7 times, join with sl st in 3rd ch of beg ch-4—8 dc and 8 ch-1 sps, do not turn.

RND 2: Ch 3 (counts as dc), dc in same ch as joining, ch 2, [2 dc in next dc, ch 2] 7 times, join with sl st in 3rd ch of beg ch-3—16 dc and 8 ch-2 sps, do not turn.

RND 3: Ch 5 (counts as dc and ch-2 sp), [dc in next dc, ch 2] 15 times, join with sl st in 3rd ch of beg ch-5—16 dc and 16 ch-2 sps, do not turn.

RND 4: Ch 3, dc in same ch as joining, 2 dc in next ch-2 sp, [2 dc in next dc, 2 dc in next ch-2 sp] 15 times, join with sl st in 3rd ch of beg ch-3—64 dc, do not turn.

RND 5: Ch 8 (counts as tr and ch-4 sp), tr in same ch as joining, *skip next 3 sts, (tr, ch 4, tr) in next st; rep from * around, skip last 3 sts, join with sl st in 4th ch of beg ch-8—32 tr and 16 ch-4 sps, do not turn.

RND 6: Ch 4 (counts as tr), tr in next tr, ch 5, [tr in each of next 2 tr, ch 5] 15 times, join with sl st in 4th ch of beg ch-4—32 tr and 16 ch-5 sps, do not turn.

RND 7: Ch 4, tr in next tr, 5 tr in next ch-5 sp, [tr in each of next 2 tr, 5 tr in next ch-5 sp] 15 times, join with sl st in 4th ch of beg ch-4—112 tr, do not turn.

RND 8: Rep Rnd 5—56 tr and 28 ch-4 sps, do not turn.

RND 9: Ch 4, tr in next tr, ch 4, [tr in each of next 2 tr, ch 4] 27 times; join with sl st in 4th ch of beg ch-4—56 tr and 28 ch-4 sps, do not turn.

RND 10: Ch 4, tr in next tr, 4 tr in next ch-4 sp, [tr in each of next 2 tr, 4 tr in next ch-4 sp] 27 times; join with sl st in 4th ch of beg ch-4—168 tr, do not turn.

Place piece between 2 layers of kitchen towel and roll with rolling pin to block bottom. Continue with rest of bowl.

RND 11: Ch 7 (counts as tr and ch-3 sp), tr in same ch as joining, [skip next 3 sts, (tr, ch 3, tr) in next st] 41 times, skip last 3 sts; join with sl st in 4th ch of beg ch-7—84 tr and 42 ch-3 sps, do not turn.

RND 12: Ch 4, tr in next tr, ch 3, [tr in each of next 2 tr, ch 3] 41 times, join with sl st in 4th ch of beg ch-4—84 tr and 42 ch-3 sps, do not turn.

RND 13: Ch 3, tr in next tr, 3 tr in next ch-3 sp, [tr dec over next 2 tr, 3 tr in next ch-3 sp] 41 times; join with sl st in top of beg tr dec—168 tr, do not turn.

RND 14: Rep Rnd 11, do not turn.

RND 15: Rep Rnd 12, ch 1, turn.

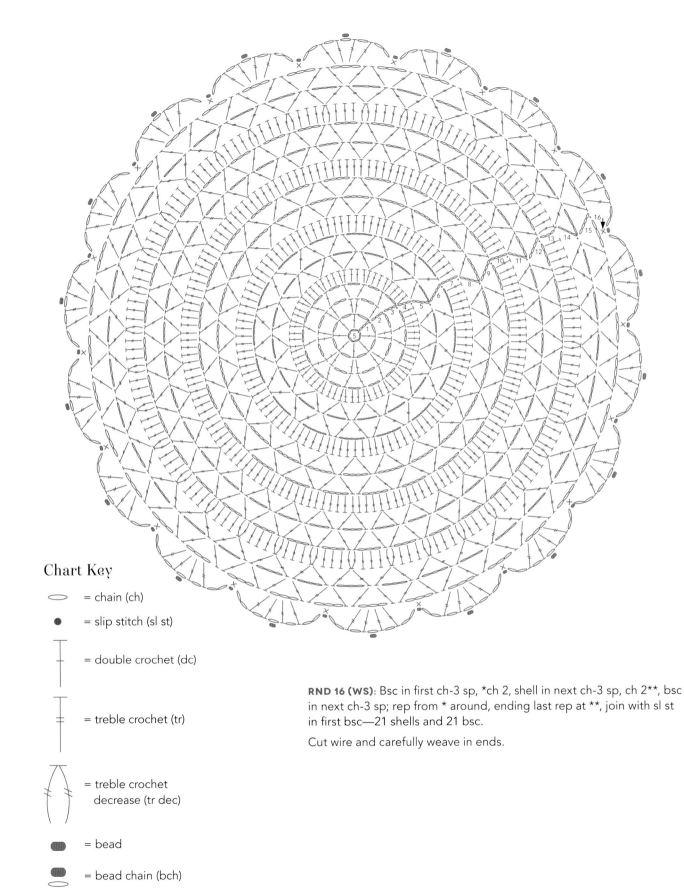

Chart Key

◯ = chain (ch)

● = slip stitch (sl st)

┬ = double crochet (dc)

╪ = treble crochet (tr)

⟨⟩ = treble crochet decrease (tr dec)

▬ = bead

▬ / ◯ = bead chain (bch)

▬ / ✕ = bead single crochet (bsc)

RND 16 (WS): Bsc in first ch-3 sp, *ch 2, shell in next ch-3 sp, ch 2**, bsc in next ch-3 sp; rep from * around, ending last rep at **, join with sl st in first bsc—21 shells and 21 bsc.

Cut wire and carefully weave in ends.

stitchy nesting dolls

SIZE

Large Doll: bottom = 1¾" (4.5 cm) tall; top = 3¾" (9.5 cm) tall.

Medium Doll: bottom = 1½" (3.8 cm) tall; top = 2¼" (5.5 cm) tall.

Small Doll: bottom = 1¼" (3.2 cm) tall; top = 1¾" (4.5 cm) tall.

Baby Doll: 1⅜" (3.5 cm) tall.

YARN

Worsted weight (#4 Medium).

Shown here: Lion Brand Yarn Vanna's Choice (170 yd [156 m]/3.5 oz [100 g]), in #109 Colonial Blue (A), #110 Navy (B), #123 Beige (C), #126 Chocolate (D), #134 Terracotta (E), #144 Magenta (F), #147 Purple (G), #171 Fern (H), #158 Mustard (I), #180 Cranberry (J), 1 skein each.

HOOK

Size 4 (3.5 mm), or size needed to obtain gauge.

Continued on next page
↓

Inspired by traditional wooden Russian matryoshka dolls, these crocheted lovelies are even cuter than the originals that inspired them! They are crocheted amigurumi-style with hand-embroidered accents.

DESIGNED BY AMY GAINES

NOTIONS

Stitch marker; tapestry needle; black round acrylic beads (for eyes), one hole, sizes 2mm (small) and 4mm (large), 2 beads each size; 3mm (medium), 4 beads; pink felt, 9" × 12" (23 × 30.5 cm), 1 sheet; small amount of fiberfill; sewing thread, in colors black (for eyes), red (for mouths), and pink (for cheeks); sewing needle.

GAUGE

10 sc and 10 rows = 2" (5 cm) in sc stitch. *Take time to check your gauge.*

STITCH GUIDE

Sc2tog
(single crochet two together)

Insert hook in next stitch, yarn over and pull up loop (2 loops on hook), insert hook in next stitch, yarn over and pull up loop (3 loops on hook), yarn over and draw through all 3 loops on hook.

Daisy Stitch (embroidery)
See Techniques.

French Knot (embroidery)
See Techniques.

Straight Stitch (embroidery)
See Techniques.

NOTES

❧ Each pattern is worked in a spiral. Place stitch marker on the last stitch of each round to mark the end of the round. Move marker up each round.

❧ When starting each pattern, use your preferred method for making the ring, leaving a 6" (15 cm) tail: (a) adjustable ring (single or double), or (b) chain 2, then start Rnd 1 in 2nd chain from hook.

large doll

BOTTOM

With color B, make a ring.

RND 1: Sc 6 times into ring—6 sc, pm in last stitch of rnd, do not turn. Cont to move marker up each rnd.

RND 2: 2 Sc in each of 6 sc—12 sc, do not turn.

RND 3: *2 Sc in next st, sc in next st; rep from * around—18 sc, do not turn.

RND 4: *2 Sc in next st, sc in each of next 2 sts; rep from * around—24 sc, do not turn.

RND 5: *2 Sc in next st, sc in each of next 3 sts; rep from * around—30 sc, do not turn.

RND 6: *2 Sc in next st, sc in each of next 4 sts; repeat around—36 sc, do not turn.

RND 7: *Working in back loops only,* sc in each st around, do not turn.

RND 8: * 2 Sc in next st, sc in each of next 5 sts; rep from * around—42 sc, do not turn.

RND 9: Sc in each st around, do not turn.

RND 10: * 2 Sc in next st, sc in each of next 6 sts; rep from * around—48 sc, do not turn.

RNDS 11-13: Sc in each st around, do not turn.

RND 14: *Sc2tog, sc in next each of next 6 sts; rep from * around—42 sc, do not turn.

RND 15: *Working in back loops only,* sc in each st around—42 sc, do not turn.

RND 16: Sc in each st around, sl st in next st, fasten off, leaving a 6" (15 cm) tail. Weave in yarn tail.

TOP

With color J, make a ring.

RNDS 1-4: Rep Rnds 1–4 of bottom—24 sc, do not turn.

RND 5: *Working in back loops only,* sc in each st around, do not turn.

RNDS 6 AND 7: Rep Rnds 5 and 6 of bottom—36 sc, do not turn.

RNDS 8-15: Sc in each st around, do not turn.

RND 16: Rep Rnd 8 of bottom—42 sc, do not turn.

RND 17: Rep Rnd 10 of bottom—48 sc, do not turn.

RNDS 18-20: Sc in each st around, do not turn.

RND 21: *Working in back loops only,* sc in each st around, do not turn.

RND 22: Sc in each st around, do not turn, sl st in next st, fasten off, leaving a 6" (15 cm) tail. Weave in yarn tail.

Color Key

- █ Colonial Blue (A)
- █ Terracotta (E)
- █ Magenta (F)
- █ Fern (H)
- ☐ Mustard (I)
- █ Cranberry (J)
- ❤ French knot

Large Doll
Cheek Template ½" (1.3 cm)

Medium Doll
Cheek Template ⅜" (1 cm)

Small Doll
Cheek Template ¼" (6 mm)

Baby Doll
Cheek Template ⅛" (3 mm)

Large Doll

Medium Doll

FACE

With color C, make a ring.

RNDS 1–5: Rep Rnds 1–5 of bottom, sl st in next st, fasten off, leaving a 16" (40.5 cm) tail. Yarn tail will be used to sew face piece to top.

HAIR

With color D, make a ring.

ROW 1: 2 Sc in 2nd ch from hook, hdc in each of the next 2 ch, [sc2tog] twice, hdc in each of the next 2 ch, 2 sc in last chain—10 sts, ch 1, turn.

ROW 2: 2 Sc in first st, sc in next st, hdc in each of the next 2 sts, sc2tog, hdc in each of the next 2 sts, sc in next st, 2 sc in last st—11 sts, turn.

Sl st in next st, fasten off, leaving a 16" (40.5 cm) tail, which will be used to sew hair to face.

FINISHING

Arrange hair piece placing foundation edge on face edge, and sew in place with yarn tail.

With black thread and 2 large black beads, sew to face for eyes. Sew a smile with red thread. Cut two ½" (1.3 cm) circles (see diagram) of pink felt for cheeks. Sew to face with pink thread.

Arrange embellished face with hair edge along Rnd 5 of top and sew in place. Embroider flowers below face and along edge following diagram for Large Doll; use daisy stitch for flowers, French knot for centers, and straight stitch for stems.

COLOR STRATEGY: PALETTE INSPIRATION

Ever notice how some people just seem to have a knack for combining colors in a way you'd never think of yourself? While it's true that some folks do have a great eye for colorwork, it's easy to fake it if you don't already have the knack. Simply find a colorful item that you love—it can be a painting, a photograph, a flowering plant, or a fabric print. Then, simply look at all the colors in that piece, and choose yarns to match. You'll be amazed at how easy it is to compile unexpected color combinations that are infinitely eye-pleasing.

medium doll

BOTTOM

With color I, make a ring.

RND 1: Sc 6 times into ring—6 sc, pm in last stitch of rnd, do not turn. Cont to move marker up each rnd.

RND 2: 2 sc in each of 6 sc—12 sc, do not turn.

RND 3: *2 Sc in next st, sc in next st; rep from * around—18 sc, do not turn.

RND 4: *2 Sc in next st, sc in each of next 2 sts; rep from * around—24 sc, do not turn.

RND 5: *Working in back loops only*, sc in each st around, do not turn.

RND 6: *2 Sc in next st, sc in each of next 3 sts; rep from * around—30 sc, do not turn.

RND 7: Sc in each st around, do not turn.

RND 8: *2 Sc in next st, sc in each of next 4 sts; repeat around—36 sc, do not turn.

RNDS 9–11: Sc in each st around, do not turn.

RND 12: *Sc2tog, sc in each of next 4 sts; rep from * around—30 sc, do not turn.

RND 13: *Working in back loops only*, sc in each st around, do not turn.

RND 14: Sc in each st around, sl st in next stitch, fasten off, leaving 6" (15 cm) tail. Weave in yarn tail.

TOP

With color H, make a ring.

RNDS 1–3: Rep Rnds 1–3 of bottom.

RND 4: *Working in back loops only*, sc in each st around, do not turn.

RND 5: Rep Rnd 4 of bottom.

RND 6: Rep Rnd 6 of bottom.

RNDS 7–12: Sc in each st around, do not turn.

RND 13: Rep Rnd 8 of bottom.

RNDS 14 AND 15: Sc in each st around, do not turn.

RND 16: *Working in back loops only*, sc in each st around, do not turn.

RND 17: Sc in each st around, sl st in next st, fasten off, leaving a 6" (15 cm) tail. Weave in yarn tail.

FACE

With color C, make a ring.

RNDS 1–4: Rep Rnds 1–4 of bottom, sl st in next st, fasten off, leaving a 16" (40.5 cm) tail, which will be used to sew face piece to top.

HAIR

With color D, ch 9.

ROW 1: 2 Sc 2nd ch from the hook, hdc in each of next 2 ch, sc2tog, hdc in each of next 2 ch, 2 sc in last ch—9 sts, ch 1, turn.

ROW 2: 2 Sc in first st, sc in next st, hdc in each of next 2 sts, sl st in next st, hdc in each of next 2 sts, sc in next st, 2 sc in last st—11 sts, turn.

Sl st in next st, fasten off, leaving 16" (40.5 cm) tail, which will be used to sew hair to face piece.

FINISHING

Arrange hair piece placing foundation edge on face edge, and sew in place with yarn tail.

With black thread and 2 medium black beads, sew to face for eyes. Sew a smile with red thread. Cut two 3/8" (1 cm) circles (see diagram) of pink felt for cheeks. Sew to face with pink thread.

With color A, sew straight stitches to embroider around face edge, and make a little bow in the center under the face.

Arrange embellished face with hair edge along Rnd 4 of top and sew in place. Embroider flowers below face and along edge following diagram for Medium Doll using daisy stitch for flowers and French knot for centers.

small doll

BOTTOM

With color G, make a ring.

RND 1: Sc 6 times into ring—6 sc, pm in last stitch of rnd, do not turn. Cont to move marker up each rnd.

RND 2: 2 Sc in each of 6 sc—12 sc, do not turn.

RND 3: *Working in back loops only,* sc in each st around, do not turn.

RND 4: *2 Sc in next st, sc in next st; rep from * around—18 sc, do not turn.

RND 5: Sc in each st around, do not turn.

RND 6: *2 Sc in next st, sc in each of next 2 sts; rep from * around—24 sc, do not turn.

RNDS 7 AND 8: Sc in each st around, do not turn.

RND 9: *Sc2tog, sc in each of next 2 sc; rep from * around—18 sts, do not turn.

RND 10: *Working in back loops only,* sc in each st around, do not turn.

Sl st in next st, fasten off, leaving 6" (15 cm) tail. Weave in yarn tail.

Color Key

■	Colonial Blue (A)
■	Terracotta (E)
■	Magenta (F)
■	Fern (H)
□	Mustard (I)
■	Cranberry (J)
⬤	French knot

Baby Doll

Small Doll

TOP

With color E, make a ring.

RNDS 1–4: Rep Rnds 1–4 of bottom.

RNDS 5–9: Sc in each st around, do not turn.

RND 10: *2 Sc in next st, sc in each of next 2 sts; rep from * around—24 sc, do not turn.

RND 11: *Working in back loops only,* sc in each st around, do not turn.

RND 12: Sc in each st around, do not turn.

Sl st in next st, fasten off, leaving 6" (15 cm) tail. Weave in yarn tail.

FACE

With color C, make a ring.

RNDS 1 AND 2: Rep Rnds 1 and 2 of bottom.

RND 3: *2 Sc in next st, sc in next st; rep from * around—18 sts, do not turn.

Sl st in next st, fasten off, leaving 16" (40.5 cm) tail, which will be used to sew face to top.

HAIR

With color D, ch 9.

ROW 1: 2 Sc in 2nd ch from hook, hdc in each of next 2 ch, sc2tog, hdc in each of next 2 ch, 2 sc in last ch—9 sts, turn.

Sl st in next st, fasten off, leaving 16" (40.5 cm) tail, which will be used to sew hair to face.

FINISHING

Arrange hair piece placing foundation edge on face edge, and sew in place with yarn tail.

With black thread and 2 medium black beads, sew to face for eyes. Sew a smile with red thread. Cut two ¼" (6 mm) circles (see diagram) of pink felt for cheeks. Sew to face with pink thread. Arrange embellished face with hair edge along Rnd 3 of top and sew in place. Split yarn to embroider flowers below face and along edge by following diagram for Small Doll using daisy stitch for flowers and French knot for centers.

baby doll

BODY

With color A, make a ring.

RND 1: Sc 5 times into ring—5 sc, pm in last stitch of rnd, do not turn. Cont to move marker up each rnd.

RND 2: 2 Sc in each of 5 sc—10 sc, do not turn.

RNDS 3 AND 4: Sc in each st around, do not turn.

RND 5: *2 Sc in next sc, sc in next sc; rep from * around—15 sc, do not turn.

RNDS 6 AND 7: Sc in each st around, fasten off yarn, do not turn.

Change to color F.

RND 8: Sc in each st around, do not turn.

Stuff with fiberfill as you work.

RND 9: *Sc2tog, sc in next st; rep from * around—10 sc, do not turn.

RND 10: *Sc2tog; rep from * around—5 sc.

Sl st in next st, fasten off, leaving 6" (15 cm) tail. Weave in yarn tail.

FACE

With color C, make a ring.

RND 1: Sc 6 times into ring—6 sc.

Sl st in next st, fasten off, leaving 16" (40.5 cm) tail, which will be used to sew face to top.

HAIR

With color D, ch 4, fasten off, leaving 16" (40.5 cm) tail, which will be used to sew hair to face.

FINISHING

Arrange hair piece placing along top edge of face and sew in place with yarn tail.

With black thread and 2 small black beads, sew to face for eyes. Sew a smile with red thread. Cut two 1/8" (3 mm) circles (see diagram) of pink felt for cheeks. Sew to face with pink thread. Arrange embellished face with hair edge along Rnd 10 of top and sew in place. Split yarn to embroider flowers below face, from bottom edge up along side by following diagram for Small Doll using daisy stitch for flowers, French knot for centers, and straight stitch for stems.

snowflake & owl buntings

SIZE
Each garland measures about 6' (1.8 m) long. Snowflakes vary slightly in size and measure from 4½" (11.5 cm) to 5" (12.5 cm) in diameter. Owls measure about 4½" (11.5 cm) tall × 3" (7.5 cm) wide.

YARN
Worsted weight (#4 Medium).

Shown here: Stitch Nation Full o' Sheep by Debbie Stoller (100% Peruvian wool; 155 yd [141 m]/3.5 oz [100 g]):

Snowflakes: in #2205 Little Lamb (A), #2510 Aquamarine (B), and #2529 Mediterranean (C), 1 skein each.

Owls: in #2925 Passion Fruit (A), #2550 Plummy (B), #2705 Peony (C), #2910 Poppy (D), #2260 Clementine (E), #2605 Honeycomb (F), and #2205 Little Lamb (G), 1 skein each.

HOOK
Size 7 (4.5 mm), or size needed to obtain gauge.

NOTIONS
Tapestry needle.

GAUGE
Gauge is not critical to this project; refer to Size for measurements of each motif.

Decorate a child's room, your craft room, or a party landscape with these cheery garlands. Choose from quick-to-make snowflakes or quirky, colorful owls. Each motif takes only a little bit of yarn, making this a great project for using up worsted weight scraps.

DESIGNED BY LINDA PERMANN

STITCH GUIDE

Picot

Ch 3, slip st in 3rd ch from hook.

**Tr2tog
(treble crochet two together)**

*Yarn over twice, insert hook in indicated st and draw up a loop, [yarn over and draw through 2 loops] twice; repeat from * once more in same st (3 loops on hook), yarn over and draw through all 3 loops on hook.

**Tr3tog
(treble crochet three together)**

*Yarn over twice, insert hook in indicated st and draw up a loop, [yarn over and draw through 2 loops] twice; repeat from * twice more in same st (4 loops on hook), yarn over and draw through all 4 loops on hook.

Blo Back loop only

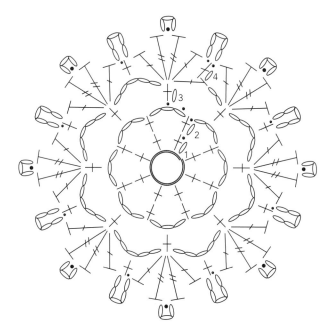

Snowflake A

snowflake garland

SNOWFLAKE A

(Make 3.)

With A, make an adjustable ring.

RND 1 (RS): Ch 1, 8 sc in ring, join with sl st in first sc—8 sc, do not turn.

RND 2: Ch 1, (sc, ch 3) in first st, (sc, ch 3) in each sc around, join with sl st in first sc—8 sc, 8 ch-3 sps, do not turn.

RND 3: Sl st in first 2 chs, ch 1, sc in same ch-sp, ch 5, *sc in next ch-3 sp, ch 5; rep from * 5 times more, sc in last ch-3 sp, (ch 2, join with a dc in first sc of rnd—counts as ch-5 sp)—8 sc, 8 ch-5 sps, do not turn.

RND 4: Ch 1, sc around post of dc just made, ch 5, sl st in same sc, (dc, tr, picot, tr, dc) in next sc, *sc in next ch-5 sp, ch 5, sl st in sc just made, (dc, tr, picot, tr, dc) in next sc, rep from * around, join with sl st in first sc—8 picots, 8 ch-5 sps.

Fasten off and weave in ends.

SNOWFLAKE B

(Make 3.)

With B, make an adjustable ring.

RND 1 (RS): Ch 3, tr2tog, ch 3, work 3 picots, ch 3, [tr3tog, ch 3, work 3 picots, ch 3] 5 times more, join with sl st in first tr2tog—6 tr3tog, six 3-picot groups.

Fasten off and weave in ends.

Snowflake B

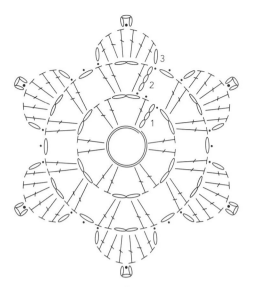

Snowflake C

Chart Key

◠ = chain (ch)

• = slip stitch (sl st)

┼ = single crochet (sc)

┼ = double crochet (dc)

┼ = treble crochet (tr)

⬥ = treble 3 together (tr3tog)

◠◠ = picot

✕✕ = 2 sc in same st

⌒ = back loop only (BLO)

SNOWFLAKE C

(Make 3.)

With C, make an adjustable ring.

RND 1 (RS): Ch 3 (counts as dc, here and throughout), dc in ring, ch 2, [2 dc in ring, ch 2] 5 times, join with sl st in top of beg ch-3—12 dc, 6 ch-2 sps, do not turn.

RND 2: Sl st in next dc and in ch-2 sp, ch 3, (dc, ch 2, 2 dc) in same ch-2 sp, ch 1, skip next 2 dc, *(2 dc, ch 2, 2 dc) in next ch-2 sp, ch 1, skip next 2 dc; rep from * around, join with sl st in beg ch—24 dc, 6 ch-2 sps, 6 ch-1 sps, do not turn.

RND 3: *Ch 1, dc in next dc, (2 dc, picot, 2 dc) in next ch-2 sp, dc in next dc, ch 1, sl st in next 3 sts; rep from * around—6 picots.

Fasten off and weave in ends.

GARLAND CHAIN

Holding strands A and B together as one and leaving a 6" (15 cm) tail, chain until strand measures about 6' (1.82 m). Fasten off, leaving 6" (15 cm) tail.

FINISHING

For best results, block snowflakes before assembling garland. Thread snowflakes onto chain through picots, chain loops, or space below picots, in the following order: B, A, C. Fold each end of garland back on itself to form a small hanging loop, and use yarn ends to sew loop in place. Space snowflakes as desired and weave in ends.

Chart Key

- ⬯ = chain (ch)
- • = slip stitch (sl st)
- + = single crochet (sc)
- ⊤ = double crochet (dc)
- ‡ = treble crochet (tr)
- ◊ = treble 3 together (tr3tog)
- ⬮ = picot
- ⤬ = 2 sc in same st
- ⌢ = back loop only (BLO)

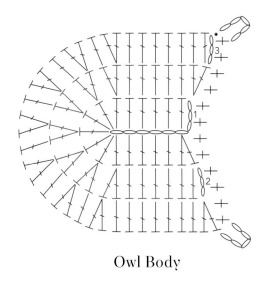

Owl Body

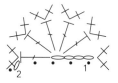

Owl Wing

Owl Eye

owl garland

OWL BODY

(Make 2 each in A, B, C, and D and 1 each in E and F.)

Ch 9.

ROW 1 (RS): Dc in 4th ch from hook (skipped 3 chs counts as first dc), dc in next 4 chs, 7 dc in next ch, turn to work across opposite side of foundation chain, dc in next 4 chs, 2 dc in last ch—19 dc, ch 3 (counts as dc here and throughout), turn.

ROW 2 (WS): Dc in first dc [increase made], dc in next 5 dc, 2 dc in each of next 7 dc, dc in next 5 dc, 2 dc in last dc—28 dc, turn.

RND 3 (RS): Ch 3, dc in first dc, dc in each of next 6 dc, [2 dc in next dc, dc in next dc] 7 times, dc in next 6 dc, 2 dc in last dc, ch 5, continuing work across top edge of owl, evenly work 12 sc across owl top, ch 5, join with sl st in top of beg ch-3—37 dc, 12 sc, 2 ch-5 lps.

Fasten off and weave in ends.

OWL EYES

(Make 12 with A centers and 8 with B centers.)

With first color (A or B), make an adjustable ring.

RND 1 (RS): Ch 1, 6 sc in ring, join with sl st in first sc—6 sc, do not turn. Fasten off first color.

RND 2 (RS): Join G in blo of any st, ch 1, 2 sc in each st around, join with sl st in first sc—12 sc. Fasten off second color, leaving a 10" (25.5 cm) tail for sewing eye to owl.

OWL BEAK

(Make 2 in D, 3 in E, and 5 in F.)

Make an adjustable ring.

ROW 1 (RS): Ch 3, 2 dc in ring—3 dc.

Fasten off, leaving a 10" (25.5 cm) tail for sewing beak to owl.

OWL WINGS

(Make 2 each in A and D and 4 each in B, C, E, and F.)

Make an adjustable ring.

ROW 1 (WS): Ch 3 (counts as dc), 5 dc in ring—6 dc, ch 1, turn.

ROW 2 (RS): 2 Sc in each dc across, sl st evenly down straight edge of wing, join with sl st in first sc—12 sc.

Fasten off, leaving a 12" (30.5 cm) tail for sewing wing to body.

OWL ASSEMBLY CHART

BODY	BEAK	EYE CENTER	WING	WING POSITION
A (make 2)	F	B	C	out
B (make 2)	D	A	E	out
C (make 2)	F	A	B	in
D (make 2)	E	A	F	in
E (make 1)	F	B	A	in
F (make 1)	E	B	D	out

FINISHING

For best results, block all pieces before assembling owls, and let dry completely. Assemble pieces according to color assembly chart. Sew eyes to center top of owl body, using the outside edge of eye as a guide for sewn stitches and inserting needle just under the V of each stitch. Repeat for beak and wings, alternating position of wings as directed by chart, or as desired. Weave in ends.

Holding strands A and B together as one, chain until strand measures about 6' (1.82 m). Fasten off, leaving 6" (15 cm) tail. Thread all owls onto strand in the following order: C, B, D, A, E, F, C, B, D, A. Thread garland strand through both ch-5 loops at top of each owl. Fold each end of garland back on itself to form a small hanging loop, and use yarn ends to sew both loops in place. Space owls as desired and weave in ends.

sleepy kitty doorstop

SIZE
9" (23 cm) long × 6" (15 cm)
deep × 5" (12.5) tall.

YARN
Worsted weight (#4 Medium).

Shown here: Red Heart Super
Saver Solid (100% acrylic; 364 yd
[333 m]/7 oz [198 g]), in #0885
Delft Blue (MC) and #0672
Spring Green (CC), ½ skein each.

HOOK
Size G/6 (4 mm), or size needed
to obtain gauge.

Steel hook size US 6 (1.6 mm),
eyes, and mouth (see notes on
page 50).

NOTIONS
Removable stitch marker;
tapestry needle; polyester
fiberfill stuffing; flat glass gems
(see notes below) or other heavy
stuffing material, between 2
and 3 lbs; 1 nylon stocking
(see notes below); 1 twist tie
(optional—see notes below);
sewing pins; DMC embroidery
floss, #820 Dk. Royal Blue, 2 yd
(1.82 m), for eyes and mouth;
DMC embroidery floss, #3824
Lt. Apricot, 1 yard (0.91 m), for
nose; embroidery needle.

Continued on next page
↓

It doesn't get any cuter than this sweet
little amigurumi kitty. Filled with glass
beads, she makes a charming doorstop,
but stuffed with fiberfill she'd make a
purrrfect plush toy, too.

DESIGNED BY BRENDA K. B. ANDERSON

GAUGE

6 rnds in sc stitch = 3" (7.5 cm) in diameter using size G/6 (4 mm) hook.

Note: Stitches should not be loose, but tight enough to create a sturdy fabric that can be stuffed firmly.

NOTES

Working in joined rounds

❖ At the end of each round, make a slip stitch to join each round. The first stitch of the next round will always be made into the same stitch as the one that the join was made into.

Changing color

❖ Make last yarn over of the previous round (this would be the yarn over in the joining slip stitch) with the new color. Do not fasten off yarn when changing colors, but carry it up inside of kitty body. Pull up new color so that it crosses over old color on the inside of kitty body.

Stuffing

❖ The doorstop must be stuffed with something heavy enough to keep it stationary. Glass gems were used, which are available at most craft stores in the floral or bridal department. Using pebbles or gravel is another option. Rice or dried beans is not suggested if doorstop will be used in an area (such as your kitchen) that might get wet.

❖ Use a nylon stocking to keep your filling in place. Or, if glass gems are packaged inside a stretchy mesh bag (if you bought the gems in a 3 lb bag), the mesh bag can be used instead of the nylon stocking.

STITCH GUIDE

Sc2tog
(single crochet two together)

Insert hook in next stitch, yarn over and pull up loop (2 loops on hook), insert hook in next stitch, yarn over and pull up loop (3 loops on hook), yarn over and draw through all 3 loops on hook.

Satin Stitch (embroidery)

See Techniques.

doorstop

BODY AND TAIL

With MC and larger hook, make an adjustable loop,

RND 1: 6 Sc into ring, join with sl st in first sc, (pull yarn tail to close loop)—6 sts, do not turn.

RND 2: Ch 1, (start in same st as the join, now and throughout body) 2 sc into each st around, join with sl st in first sc—12 sts, do not turn.

RND 3: Ch 1, [1 sc in next st, 2 sc in next st] 6 times, join with sl st in first sc—18 sts, do not turn.

RND 4: Ch 1, [1 sc in each of next 2 sts, 2 sc in next st] 6 times, join with sl st in first sc—24 sts, do not turn.

RND 5: Ch 1, [1 sc in each of next 3 sts, 2 sc in next st] 6 times, join with sl st in first sc—30 sts, do not turn.

RND 6: Ch 1, [1 sc in each of next 4 sts, 2 sc in next st] 6 times, join with sl st in first sc—36 sts, do not turn.

RND 7: Ch 1, [1 sc in each of next 6 sts, 2 sc in next st, 1 sc in each of next 5 sts] 3 times, join with sl st in first sc—39 sts, do not turn.

RND 8: Ch 1, [1 sc in each of next 12 sts, 2 sc in next st] 3 times, join with sl st in first sc—42 sts, do not turn.

RND 9: Ch 1, [1 sc in next 2 sts, 2 sc in next st, 1 sc in next 11 sts] 3 times, join with sl st in first sc—45 sts, do not turn.

RND 10: Ch 1, [1 sc in each of next 10 sts, 2 sc in next st, 1 sc in each of next 4 sts] 3 times, join with sl st in first sc—48 sts, do not turn.

RND 11: Ch 1, [1 sc in each of next 7 sts, 2 sc in next st, 1 sc in each of next 8 sts] 3 times, join with sl st in first sc—51 sts, do not turn.

RND 12: Ch 1, [1 sc in each of next 13 sts, 2 sc in next st, 1 sc in each of next 3 sts] 3 times, join with sl st in first sc changing to CC on last yo—54 sts, do not turn.

RNDS 13-15 AND 21-23: Ch 1, 1 sc in each st, join with sl st in first sc changing to MC on last yo of Rnd 15 (23), do not turn.

RNDS 16-20 AND 24-28: Ch 1, 1 sc in each st, join with sl st in first sc changing to CC on last yo of Rnd 20 (28), do not turn.

RNDS 29-31: Ch 1, 1 sc in each st, join with sl st in first sc changing to MC on last yo of Rnd 31, do not turn.

RND 32: Ch 1, [1 sc in each of next 13 sts, sc2tog, 1 sc in each of next 3 sts] 3 times, join with sl st in first sc—51 sts, do not turn.

RND 33: Ch 1, [1 sc in each of next 7 sts, sc2tog, 1 sc in each of next 8 sts] 3 times, join with sl st in first sc—48 sts, do not turn.

RND 34: Ch 1, [1 sc in each of next 10 sts, sc2tog, 1 sc in each of next 4 sts] 3 times, join with sl st in first sc—45 sts, do not turn.

RND 35: Ch 1, [1 sc in each of next 2 sts, sc2tog, 1 sc in each of next 11 sts] 3 times, join with sl st in first sc—42 sts, do not turn.

RND 36: Ch 1, [1 sc in each of next 12 sts, sc2tog] 3 times, join with sl st in first sc—39 sts, do not turn.

RND 37: Ch 1, [1 sc in each of next 6 sts, sc2tog, 1 sc in each of next 5 sts] 3 times, join with sl st in first sc—36 sts, do not turn, do not fasten off. Set aside.

Fill the toe of stocking with as much heavy filling as will fit inside the body (leaving a little room for a bit of fiberfill around all sides). Cut the stocking with enough extra length to tie into a knot. Either use a twist tie or loosely knot the end of the nylon stocking, so that you can reopen the stocking to adjust the amount of filling as your work progresses. Place some fiberfill in the end of body and then place the filled stocking into the body. Using fiberfill, pad around all sides of the stocking, making it as smooth as possible. Continue constructing Kitty's body, adjusting the filling as needed.

RND 38: Ch 1, [1 sc in each of next 2 sts, sc2tog, 1 sc in each of next 2 sts] 6 times, join with sl st in first sc—30 sts, do not turn.

RND 39: Ch 1, [1 sc in each of next 3 sts, sc2tog] 6 times, join with sl st in first sc—24 sts, do not turn, do not fasten off.

Permanently tie the end of stocking. Stuff the body and tail firmly with fiberfill as work progresses.

RND 40: Ch 1, [1 sc in next st, sc2tog, 1 sc in next st] 6 times, join with sl st in first sc—18 sts, do not turn.

RNDS 41–50: Ch 1, 1 sc in each st, join with sl st in first sc changing to CC on last yo of Rnd 50, do not turn.

RND 51: Ch 1, 1 sc in each of next 16 sts, sc2tog, join with sl st in first sc—17 sts, do not turn.

RNDS 52 AND 53: Ch 1, 1 sc in each st, join with sl st in first sc changing to MC on last yo of Rnd 53, do not turn.

RNDS 54–56: Ch 1, 1 sc in each st, join with sl st in first sc changing to CC on last yo of Rnd 56, do not turn.

RND 57: Ch 1, 1 sc in each of next 15 sts, sc2tog, join with sl st in first sc—16 sts, do not turn.

RNDS 58 AND 59: Ch 1, 1 sc in each st, join with sl st in first sc changing to MC on last yo of Rnd 59, do not turn.

RNDS 60–62: Ch 1, 1 sc in each st, join with sl st in first sc changing to CC on last yo of Rnd 62, do not turn.

RND 63: Ch 1, 1 sc in each of next 14 sts, sc2tog, join with sl st in first sc—15 sts, do not turn.

RNDS 64 AND 65: Ch 1, 1 sc in each st, join with sl st in first sc changing to MC on last yo of Rnd 65, do not turn.

RNDS 66–68: Ch 1, 1 sc in each st, join with sl st in first sc changing to CC on last yo of Rnd 68.

RND 69: Ch 1, 1 sc in each of next 13 sts, sc2tog, join with sl st in first sc—14 sts, do not turn.

RNDS 70 AND 71: Ch 1, 1 sc in each st, join with sl st in first sc changing to MC on last yo of Rnd 71, do not turn.

RNDS 72-74: Ch 1, 1 sc in each st, join with sl st in first sc changing to CC on last yo of Rnd 74, do not turn.

RND 75: Ch 1, 1 sc in each of next 12 sts, sc2tog, join with sl st in first sc—13 sts, do not turn.

RNDS 76-77: Ch 1, 1 sc in each st, join with sl st in first sc changing to MC on last yo of Rnd 77, do not turn.

RNDS 78-80: Ch 1, 1 sc in each st, join with sl st in first sc changing to CC on last yo of Rnd 80, do not turn.

RND 81: Ch 1, 1 sc in each of next 11 sts, sc2tog, join with sl st in first sc—12 sts, do not turn.

RNDS 82-92: Ch 1, 1 sc in each st, join with sl st in first sc, do not turn.

RND 93: Ch 1, sc2tog 6 times, join with sl st in first sc—6 sts.

Fasten off, leaving 12" (30.5 cm) tail. Thread yarn tail through front loop of 6 rem sts and pull tight to close hole. Weave in ends and set aside.

HEAD (WORKED IN SPIRAL)
With MC and larger hook, ch 7.

RND 1: In 2nd ch from hook, 1 sc in bottom bump in each of next 6 chs—6 sc, place marker to indicate beg of rnds moving marker up each rnd. (Note: The first ch from hook is a t-ch—do not work this st on the next rnd.)

RND 2: Cont around to other side of foundation chain, rotate work clockwise 180 degrees, 2 sc in first st, 1 sc in each of next 4 sts, 2 sc in next st, rotating work clockwise 180 degrees, skip t-ch from Rnd 1, 2 sc in next st, 1 sc in each of next 4 sts, 2 sc in last—16 sts.

RND 3: [2 sc in next st, 1 sc in each of next 6 sts, 2 sc in next st] twice—20 sts, sc in next st, move marker after this st to mark new beg of next rnd.

RND 4: [2 sc in next st, 1 sc in each of next 8 sts, 2 sc in next st] twice—24 sts.

RND 5: [2 sc in next st, 1 sc in each of next 10 sts, 2 sc in next st] twice—28 sts.

RND 6: [2 sc in next st, 1 sc in each of next 12 sts, 2 sc in next st] twice—32 sts, sc in next st, move marker after this st to mark new beg of next rnd.

RND 7: [2 sc in next st, 1 sc in each of next 14 sts, 2 sc in next st] twice—36 sts.

RNDS 8-15: 1 sc in each st around, sc in each of next 2 sts, move marker after these 2 sts to mark new beg of next rnd.

RND 16: [Sc2tog, 1 sc in each of next 14 sts, sc2tog] twice—32 sts.

COLOR TIP

Nontraditional kitty colors make this little creature extra cute. Have fun adding purrrsonality with your own color choices—school or sports team colors, purrrhaps?

RND 17: [Sc2tog, 1 sc in each of next 12 sts, sc2tog] twice—28 sts.

RND 18: [Sc2tog, 1 sc in each of next 10 sts, sc2tog] twice—24 sts.

Fasten off, leaving 12" (30.5 cm) tail. Stuff head with fiberfill. Sew opening at top of head closed through front loops only. Weave in ends and set aside.

EARS

(worked in spiral)

With MC and larger hook, make an adjustable loop.

RND 1: 6 Sc in loop, pull yarn tail to close loop—6 sts, place marker to indicate beg of rnds moving marker up each rnd.

RND 2: [1 sc in next st, 2 sc in next st] 3 times—9 sts.

RND 3: [1 sc in each of next 2 sts, 2 sc in next st] 3 times—12 sts.

RND 4: [1 sc in next st, 2 sc in next st, 1 sc in each of next 2 sts] 3 times—15 sts.

RND 5: [2 sc in next st, 1 sc in each of next 4 sts] 3 times—18 sts.

RND 6: [1 sc in each of next 3 sts, 2 sc in next st, 1 sc in each of next 2 sts] 3 times—21 sts.

RND 7: [1 sc in each of next 2 sts, 2 sc in next st, 1 sc in each of next 4 sts] 3 times—24 sts.

Fasten off, leaving 12" (30.5 cm) tail.

Fold ear flat and stitch the two layers together at bottom edge. Pin ears to top of head using photo as guide. The bottom edge of each ear should be shaped into a C where it meets the head. Stitch ears to head using MC. Set aside.

EYES (EMBROIDERY)

(Make 2.)

Using steel hook and blue embroidery floss, ch 11.

ROW 1: Working in bottom of chs, sl 1 st in 2nd ch from hook, and in each ch across—10 sts.

Fasten off, leaving 6" (15 cm) tail.

Using embroidery needle and tail ends, stitch each eye to face using photo as guide.

MOUTH (EMBROIDERY)

Using steel hook and blue embroidery floss, ch 15.

ROW 1: Working in bottom of chs, sl 1 st in 2nd ch from hook and in next ch, ch 12.

Fasten off, leaving 6" (15 cm) tail.

Using embroidery needle and tail ends, stitch mouth to face using photo as guide. The slip-stitch section of the mouth should point upward to the bottom of the nose.

NOSE (EMBROIDERY)

Using embroidery needle and apricot embroidery floss, satin stitch (with vertical stitches) a triangular nose in place just above the mouth. Add a few horizontal satin stitches across the top of nose. Using blue embroidery floss, embroider a couple of straight stitches along the sides of the nose to give the nose extra definition.

FINISHING

Pin tail by wrapping around side toward top of body, and stitch in place. Pin head in place just above the tail, angled slightly (see photo), and stitch in place. Weave in ends.

tranquil
bedroom

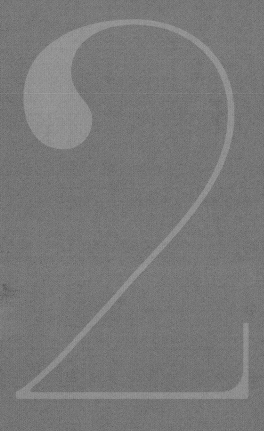

filet zigs and zags

SIZE
38" (96.5 cm) × 62" (157.5 cm), after blocking.

YARN
Sportweight (#2 Fine).

Shown here: Red Heart Luster Sheen (100% acrylic, 307 yd [281 m]/3.5 oz [100 g]), in #0615 Tea Leaf, 6 skeins.

HOOK
Size E/4 (3.5 mm), or size needed to obtain gauge.

GAUGE
21 dc and 16 rows = 4" (10 cm) over dc patt st using size E/4 (3.5 mm) hook, before blocking. *Take time to check your gauge.*

Filet crochet isn't just for flowers and lace! Worked in a chevron pattern, filet is thoroughly graphic and modern. This pattern is easy to alter to become a window curtain, for perfect custom results.

DESIGNED BY MARI LYNN PATRICK

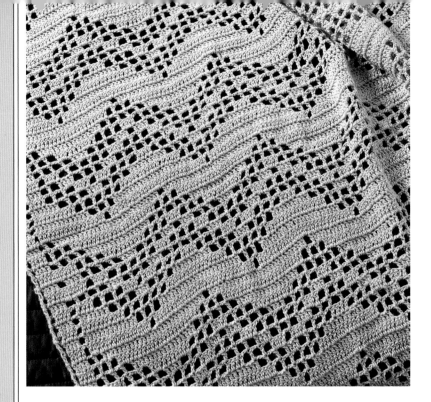

STITCH GUIDE

One Mesh (Open) Square
Ch 2, skip 2 sts, dc in next dc.

One Solid (Filled) Square
2 dc in ch-2 sp (or dc in each 2 dc in row below), dc in next dc.

NOTES

❖ The chart for the curtain represents filet mesh crochet blocks combined with "dc filled" solid blocks.

❖ To alter the width of the curtain (for 6" [15 cm] in width or 3" [7.5 cm] length), either add or subtract one patt rep and to alter the length, add or subtract one 12-row rep.

filet zigs and zags

Ch 205 evenly.

ROW 1: Dc in 7th ch from hook, *ch 2, skip 2 ch, dc in next ch; rep from * to end—67 mesh blocks, ch 5 (counts as dc and ch 2), turn.

ROW 2: Dc in next dc, *2 dc in ch-2 sp, dc in next dc; rep from * to last mesh, dc ch 2, skip last 2 ch, dc in top of tch, ch 5 (counts as dc and ch 2), turn.

ROW 3: Dc in next dc, (dc in each of next 2 dc, dc in next dc), (ch 2, skip 2 sts, dc in next dc), (dc in each of next 2 dc, dc in next dc), *(ch 2, skip 2 sts, dc in next dc); rep from * 59 times, (dc in each of next 2 dc, dc in next dc), (ch 2, skip 2 sts, dc in next dc), (dc in each of next 2 dc, dc in next dc), (ch 2, skip 2 chs, dc in next ch), ch 5 (counts as dc and ch 2), turn.

ROWS 4–24: Cont to work even foll chart with ch 5 at beg of rows as established.

Rep rows 13–24 (for the 12-row repeat) 11 times more with ch 5 at beg of rows as established.

ROWS 25-32: Cont to work even foll chart with ch 5 at beg of rows as established.

Fasten off.

FINISHING

Weave in ends. Wet block to measurements. Hang as curtain if desired.

Chart Key

☐ Mesh Square
= (ch 2, skip 2 sts,
dc in next dc).

⊡ Solid Square
= 2 dc in ch-2 sp
(or dc in each
2 dc in row below),
dc in next dc.

COLOR TIP

When it comes to color, sometimes less is more—and this
piece proves it. The intricate
pattern might get lost if
worked in multiple colors or a
variegated yarn, so to allow
an openwork stitch like this
to truly shine, stick with a
single solid shade.

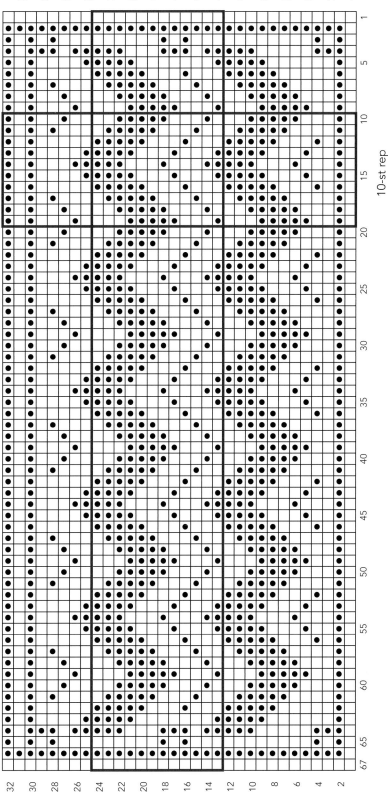

filet zigs and zags

trinket bowls

SIZES
3 round bowls measure about 3½ (4, 4½)" (9 [10, 11.5] cm) each in diameter.

3 square bowls measure about 5 (5½, 6)" (12.5 [14, 15] cm) across.

YARN
Worsted weight (#4 Medium).

Shown here: Patons Classic Wool (100% wool; 210 yd [192 m]/3.5 oz [100 g]), in #77514 Sesame (A), #00240 Leaf Green (B), #00218 Peacock (C), 1 skein each.

HOOK
Size I/9 (5.5 mm), or size needed to obtain gauge.

NOTIONS
Stitch markers; one 6 oz round glass bowl (for blocking/shaping round bowls); one 10 oz square glass bowl (for blocking/shaping square bowls).

GAUGE
16 sc and 16 rnds = 4" (10 cm), before felting.

Corral jewelry and other odds and ends in these charming felted bowls. When empty, they nest together to form a perfect set. They make a lovely small gift for a hostess or housewarming.

DESIGNED BY LINDA CYR

NOTES

✤ Instructions for smallest size are given; changes for medium and large sizes are in parentheses.

✤ When changing colors, work the last stitch with working yarn until only one step remains to complete it (e.g., for single crochet, insert hook in next stitch and pull up a loop. Drop working yarn and let it fall to the back of work, yarn over with new yarn and draw through remaining loops on hook to complete stitch. Continue with new yarn.

round bowls (worked in spiral)

Colors MC/CC: C/B (A/C, B/A)

With color MC, ch 2.

RND 1: 6 Sc in 2nd ch from hook, place marker to indicate beg of rnds moving marker up each rnd.

RND 2: 2 Sc in each sc around—12 sc.

RND 3: [Sc in next st, 2 sc in next sc] 6 times—18 sc.

RND 4: [Sc in each of next 2 sc, 2 sc in next sc] 6 times—24 sc.

RND 5: [Sc in each of next 3 sc, 2 sc in next sc] 6 times—30 sc.

RND 6: [Sc in each of next 4 sc, 2 sc in next sc] 6 times—36 sc.

RND 7 (8, 9): [Sc in each of next 5 (6, 7) sc, 2 sc in next sc] 6 times— 42 (48, 54) sc.

NEXT 2 RNDS: Sc in each sc around.

NEXT RND: [Sc in each of next 5 (7, 8) sc, 2 sc in next sc] 6 times— 48 (54, 60) sc.

NEXT 2 RNDS: Sc in each sc around, change to color CC in last rnd.

NEXT RND: Sc in each sc around.

NEXT RND: Sl st in each sc around, fasten off.

square bowls (worked in spiral)

Colors MC/CC: B/A (C/B, A/C).

With color MC, ch 2.

RND 1: 8 sc in 2nd ch from hook—8 sc, place marker to indicate beg of rnds moving marker up each rnd.

RND 2: [(Sc, ch 1, sc) in next sc, sc in next sc] 4 times—12 sc and 4 ch-1 sps.

RND 3: Sc in next sc, [(sc, ch 1, sc) in ch-1 sp, sc in each of next 3 sc] 3 times, (sc, ch 1, sc) ch-1 sp, sc in each of next 2 sc—20 sc and 4 ch-1 sps.

RND 4: Sc in each of next 2 sc, [(sc, ch 1, sc) in ch-1 sp, sc in each of next 5 sc] 3 times, (sc, ch 1, sc) in ch-1 sp, sc in each of next 3 sc—28 sc and 4 ch-1 sps.

RND 5: Sc in each of next 3 sc, [(sc, ch 1, sc) in ch-1 sp, sc in each of next 7 sc] 3 times, (sc, ch 1, sc) in ch-1 sp, sc in each of next 4 sc—36 sc and 4 ch-1 sps.

RND 6: Sc in each of next 4 sc, [(sc, ch 1, sc) in ch-1 sp, sc in each of next 9 sc] 3 times, (sc, ch 1, sc) in ch-1 sp, sc in each of next 5 sc—44 sc and 4 ch-1 sps.

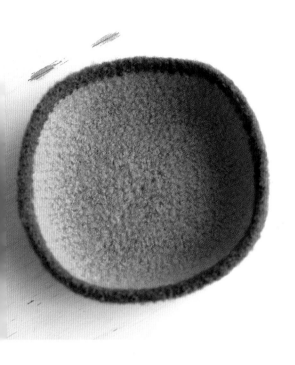

FOR MEDIUM AND LARGE SIZES ONLY

RND 7: Sc in each of next 5 sc, [(sc, ch 1, sc) in ch-1 sp, sc in each of next 11 sc] 3 times, (sc, ch 1, sc) in ch-1 sp, sc in each of next 6 sc—52 sc and 4 ch-1 sps.

FOR LARGE SIZE ONLY

RND 8: Sc in each of next 6 sc, [(sc, ch 1, sc) in ch-1 sp, sc in each of next 13 sc] 3 times, (sc, ch 1, sc) in ch-1 sp, sc in each of next 7 sc—60 sc and 4 ch-1 sps.

NEXT RND: (Sc blo) in each sc around.

NEXT RND: Sc in each sc around.

NEXT RND: Sc in each of next 5 (6, 7) sc, [(sc, ch 1, sc) in ch-1 sp, sc in each of next 11 (13, 15) sc] 3 times, (sc, ch 1, sc) in ch-1 sp, 6 (7, 8) sc—52 (60, 68) sc and 4 ch-1 sps.

NEXT 2 RNDS: Sc in each sc around.

NEXT RND: Sc in each of next 6 (7, 8) sc, [(sc, ch 1, sc) in ch-1 sp, sc in each of next 13 (15, 17) sc] 3 times, (sc, ch 1, sc) in ch-1 sp, sc in each of next 7 (8, 9) sc—60 (68, 76) sc and 4 ch-1 sps.

NEXT 2 RNDS: Sc in each sc around, change to CC in last rnd.

NEXT RND: Sc in each sc around.

NEXT RND: Sl st in each sc around, fasten off.

FINISHING

Weave in ends.

Secure and clip ends. Felt pieces using your method of choice. (Samples were felted in a front-loading washer using a heavy-duty hot/cold cycle, ¼ cup baking soda, 2 tablespoons dishwashing liquid, and old jeans for agitation.)

Stretch small round bowl piece over glass bowl. Steam with iron to set. Stretch medium round bowl piece over smallest piece (still on bowl), top should be even with base of contrast edge; steam to set. Repeat with large round piece. Allow to dry thoroughly. Repeat blocking for square bowls over square glass bowls.

chunky doily rug

SIZE
36" (91.5 cm) in diameter, after blocking.

YARN
Worsted weight (#4 Medium).

Shown here: Lion Brand Wool-Ease (80% acrylic, 20% wool, 197 yd [180 m]/3 oz [85 g]), in #620-099 Fisherman, 5 skeins.

HOOK
Size N (10 mm), or size needed to obtain gauge.

NOTIONS
Tapestry needle.

GAUGE
4½ dc and 2 rnds = 2" (5 cm) in dc stitch using 3 strands together and size N (10 mm) hook. *Take time to check your gauge.*

Think you have no patience for crocheting doilies? Think again! Stitched on a giant hook with three strands of yarn held together, this piece works up quickly and makes a major statement in any room.

DESIGNED BY PAMELA WYNNE

rug

With 3 strands of yarn tog, ch 6, join with sl st to first ch to form ring being careful not to twist ch.

RND 1: Ch 1, 8 sc in ring—8 sc, join with sl st in first sc, do not turn.

RND 2: Ch 5, [dc in next st, ch 2] 7 times, join with sl st in 3rd ch of beg ch—8 dc and 8 ch-2 sps, do not turn.

RND 3: Ch 3 (counts as dc), 2 dc in first ch-2 sp, [ch 2, 3 dc in next ch-2 sp] 7 times, ch 2, join with sl st in top of beg ch-3—24 dc and 8 ch-2 sps, do not turn.

RND 4: Ch 3 (counts as dc), dc in same sp as joining, dc in each of next 2 dc, [(dc, ch 2, dc) in next ch-2 sp, dc in each of next 3 dc] 7 times, dc in ch-2 sp, ch 2, join with sl st in top of beg ch-3—40 dc and 8 ch-2 sps, do not turn.

RND 5: Ch 3 (counts as dc), dc in same sp as joining, dc in each of next 4 dc, [(dc, ch 2, dc) in next ch-2 sp, dc in each of next 5 dc] 7 times, dc in ch-2 sp, ch 2, join with sl st in top of beg ch-3—56 dc and 8 ch-2 sps, do not turn.

RND 6: Sl st in first dc, ch 3 (counts as dc), dc in each of next 4 dc, [ch 3, skip next dc, sc in next ch-2 sp, ch 3, skip next dc, dc in each of next 5 dc] 7 times, ch 3, sc in last ch-2 sp, ch 3, join with sl st top of beg ch-3—40 dc, 8 sc and 16 ch-3 sps, do not turn.

RND 7: Sl st in first dc, ch 3 (counts as dc), dc in next 2 dc, [ch 4, skip next dc, sc in next sc, ch 4, skip next dc, dc in each of next 3 dc] 7 times, ch 4, skip next dc, sc in next sc, ch 4, join with sc in top of beg ch-3—24 dc, 8 sc and 16 ch-4 sps, do not turn.

RND 8: Ch 1, sc in same sp as joining, ch 2, skip next dc, sc in next dc, [3 sc in next ch-4 sp, ch 2, skip sc, 3 sc in next ch-4 sp, sc in next dc, ch 2, skip next dc, sc in next dc] 7 times, 3 sc in next ch 4 sp, ch 2, skip sc, 3 sc in last ch-4 sp, join with sl st in first sc—64 sc and 15 ch-2 sps, do not turn.

RND 9: Ch 3 (counts as dc), (dc ch 2, 2 dc) in first ch-2 sp, [ch 2, (dc, ch 5, dc) in next ch-2 sp, ch 2, (2 dc, ch 2, 2 dc) in next ch-2 sp] 7 times, ch 2, (dc, ch 5, dc) in last ch-2 sp, ch 2, join with sl st in top of beg ch-3, do not turn.

RND 10: Sl st in first dc and ch-2 sp, ch 3 (counts as dc), (dc, ch 2, 2 dc) in same ch-2 sp, [ch 2, skip next ch-2 sp, 6 tr in ch-5 sp, ch 2, skip next ch-2 sp, (2 dc, ch 2, 2 dc) in next ch-2 sp] 7 times, ch 2, skip next ch-2 sp, 6 tr in last ch-5 sp, ch 2, skip next ch-2 sp, join with sl st in top of beg ch-3, do not turn.

RND 11: Sl st in first dc and ch-2 sp, ch 3 (counts as dc), (dc, ch 2, 2 dc) in same ch-2 sp, [ch 2, skip next ch-2 sp, (dc, ch 1) in each of the next 5 tr, dc in next tr, ch 2, skip next ch-2 sp, (2 dc, ch 2, 2 dc) in next ch-2 sp] 7 times, ch 2, skip next ch-2 sp, (dc, ch 1) in each of the next 5 tr, dc in next tr, ch 2, skip next ch-2 sp, join with sl st to the top of beg ch-3, do not turn.

COLOR TIP

Consider the color of your floor when picking yarn for this piece. Choose a yarn in a shade that contrasts with your existing floor, to be sure the giant lace pattern will really pop.

RND 12: Sl st in first ch-2 sp, ch 3 (counts as dc), (dc, ch 2, 2 dc) in same ch-2 sp, [ch 2, skip next ch-2 sp, (sc, ch 3) in each of the next 4 ch-1 sps, sc in next ch-1 sp, ch 2, skip next ch-2 sp, (2 dc, ch 2, 2 dc) in next ch-2 sp] 7 times, ch 2, skip next ch-2 sp, (sc, ch 3) in each of the next 4 ch-1 sps, sc in next ch-1 sp, ch 2, skip last ch-2 sp, join with sl st at top of beg ch-3, join with sl st in top of beg ch-3, do not turn.

RND 13: Sl st in first dc and ch-2 sp, ch 3 (counts as dc), (dc, ch 2, 2 dc, ch 2, 2 dc) in same ch-2sp, ch 2, skip next ch-2 sp, [(sc, ch 3) in each of next 3 ch-3 sps, sc in next ch-3 sp, ch 2, skip next ch-2 sp, (2 dc, ch 2) 3 times in the next ch-2 sp, skip next ch-2 sp] 7 times, (sc, ch 3) in each of the next 3 ch-3 sps, sc in next ch-3 sp, ch 2, skip last ch-2 sp, join with a sl st in top of beg ch-3, do not turn.

RND 14: Sl st in first dc and ch-2 sp, ch 3 (counts as dc), (dc, ch 2, 2 dc) in same ch-2 sp, ch 3, (2 dc, ch 2) twice in next ch-2 sp, skip next ch-2 sp, [(sc, ch 3) in each of the next 2 ch-3 sps, sc in next ch-3 sp, ch 2, skip next ch-2 sp, (2 dc, ch 2, 2 dc) in the next ch-2 sp, ch 3, (2 dc, ch 2) twice in the next ch-2 sp, skip next ch-2 sp] 7 times, (sc, ch 3) in each of the next 2 ch-3 sps, sc in the next ch-3 sp, ch 2, skip last ch-2 sp, join with sl st in top of beg ch-3, do not turn.

RND 15: Sl st in the next dc and next ch-2 sp, ch 3 (counts as dc), (dc, ch 2, 2 dc) in same ch-2 sp, ch 3, (dc, ch 3) twice in next ch-3 sp, (2 dc, ch 2) twice in next ch-2 sp, skip next ch-2 sp, [sc in next ch-3 sp, ch 3, sc in next ch-3 sp, ch 2, skip next ch-2 sp, (2 dc, ch 2, 2 dc) in next ch-2 sp, ch 3, (dc, ch 3) twice in next ch-3 sp, (2 dc, ch 2) twice in next ch-2 sp, skip next ch-2 sp] 7 times, sc in next ch-3 sp, ch 3, sc in next ch-3 sp, ch 2, skip last ch-2 sp, join with sl st in top of beg ch-3, do not turn.

RND 16: Sl st in first dc and next ch-2 sp, ch 3 (counts as dc), (dc, ch 2, 2 dc) in same ch-2 sp, ch 3, [(dc, ch 3) twice in next ch-3 sp] 3 times, (2

COLOR STRATEGY: NEUTRAL ANCHOR

If you crave a project with a ton of color, such as a motif afghan, but you want to be sure the end result won't just look like a random hodge-podge, use one neutral color as an anchor. Black, grey, white or tan are all classic choices. You may want to use your neutral as the center and outer round of all of your motifs, or mix it in more randomly. Either way, one recurring neutral shade is a great way to tie together many disparate colors.

dc, ch 2) twice in next ch-2 sp, skip next ch-2 sp, *(sc, ch 2) in next ch-3 sp, skip next ch-2 sp, (2 dc, ch 2, 2 dc) in next ch-2 sp, ch 3, [(dc, ch 3) twice in next ch-3 sp] 3 times, (2 dc, ch 2) twice in next ch-2 sp, skip next ch-2 sp, repeat from * 6 times more, sc in next ch-3 sp, ch 2, skip last ch-2 sp, join with sl st in top of beg ch-3, do not turn.

RND 17: Ch 1, sc in first dc, sc in ch-2 sp, sc in each of next 2 dc, (2 sc in next ch-3 sp, sc in next sc) twice, 2 dc in next ch-3 sp, dc in next dc, (dc, tr, dc) in next ch-2 sp, dc in next dc, 2 dc in next ch-3 sp, (sc in next dc, 2 sc in next ch-3 sp) twice, sc in each of next 2 dc, sc in ch-2 sp, sc in each of next 2 dc, sc in next ch-2 sp, ch 1, sc in sc, ch 1, sc in next ch-2 sp, *sc in next 2 dc, sc in ch-2 sp, sc in each of next 2 dc, (2 sc in next ch-3 sp, sc in next sc) twice, 2 dc in next ch-3 sp, dc in next dc, (dc, tr, dc) in next ch-2 sp, dc in next dc, 2 dc in next ch-3 sp, (sc in next dc, 2 sc in next ch-3 sp) twice, sc in next 2 dc, sc in ch-2 sp, sc in next 2 dc, sc in next ch-2 sp, ch 1, sc in sc, ch 1, sc in next ch-2 sp; rep from * around, join with sl st in beg ch-1, do not turn.

RND 18 Ch 1, sc in same sp as joining, [ch 1, skip next st, sc in next st] 7 times, ch 1, dc in tr, ch 1, *[sc in next dc, ch 1, skip next st] 8 times, sc in sc, [ch 1, skip next st, sc in next st] 8 times, ch 1, dc in tr, ch 1; rep from * 6 times more, [sc in next dc, ch 1, skip next st] 8 times, sc in sc, ch 1, join with sl st in first sc, do not turn.

RND 19: (Sl st, 3 dc) in first ch-1 sp, (sl st in next ch-1 sp, 3 dc in next ch-1 sp) twice, *sl st in next ch-1 sp, 6 dc in next ch-1 sp, (sl st, 6 dc) next ch-1 sp, (6 dc, sl st) in next ch-1 sp), 6 dc in next ch-1 sp, (sl st in next ch-1 sp, 3 dc in next ch-1 sp) 3 times, sl st in next 2 ch-1 sps**, (3 dc in next ch-1 sp, sl st in next ch-1 sp) twice, 3 dc in next ch-1 sp; rep from * 7 times more ending last rep at **, join with st st in beg sl st, fasten off.

FINISHING
Weave in ends and block to measurements.

pinwheel baby blanket

SIZE
33" (84 cm) wide × 39" (99 cm) tall.

YARN
DK weight (#3 Light).

Shown here: Quince and Co. Chickadee (100% American wool; 181 yd [166 m]/1.75 oz [50 g]), in #135 Dogwood (A), #113 Clay (B), #114 Frank's Plum (C), #130 Split Pea (D), #120 Gingerbread (E), 2 hanks each; #104 Storm (F), 3 hanks.

HOOK
Size G/6 (4 mm), or size needed to obtain gauge.

NOTIONS
Knitting marking pins; tapestry needle.

GAUGE
1 granny square = 6" × 6" (15 × 15 cm). *Take time to check your gauge.*

Swaddle baby in a blanket stitched in soothing shades that are sophisticated enough for any décor. This is one project that's sure to become an heirloom.

DESIGNED BY ROBYN CHACHULA

STITCH GUIDE

BPsc (back post single crochet)
Insert hook from back to front to back around post of corresponding stitch below, yarn over and pull up loop, yarn over and draw through two loops on hook.

Blo Back loop only

Sc blo Single crochet in back loop only

Hdc blo Half double crochet in back loop only

NOTE

Motif Color Combinations
❖ Make 6 granny motifs in each of the following color combinations: ADF, BCF, CAF, DEF, and EBF. Change color when noted in the pattern.

Blanket

SPIRAL MOTIF (CENTER PETAL)
Make adjustable ring with first color.

RND 1 (WS): Ch 1, 16 sc in ring, sl st to first sc, pull ring closed, do not turn.

RND 2 (PETAL A): Ch 10, sl st in prev sc, ch 2 (counts as dc), skip 1 sc (on Rnd 1), sl st to next sc, turn. 3 dc in ch-10 sp, ch 2 (counts as dc), sl st in ch-10 sp, sl st in 4th ch of ch-10 from Rnd 1, sl st in each of next 3 chs of ch-10 from Rnd 1, ch 3 (counts as dc); turn. 6 dc in ch-10 sp (around sl sts), sl st to top of ch-2, do not turn. (12 dc)

RND 2 (PETAL B): Ch 7, sl st in prev sc on Rnd 1, ch 2 (counts as dc), skip 1 sc, sl st to next sc on Rnd 1, turn. 3 dc in ch-7 sp, ch 2 (counts as dc), sl st in ch-7 sp, sl st in 4th ch of ch-7, sl st in each of next 3 ch of ch-7, ch 3 (counts as dc), turn. 6 dc in ch-7 sp (around sl sts), sl st to top of ch-2, do not turn. (12 dc)

RND 2 (PETALS C–H): Rep Petal B 6 times more, sl st to Petal A, fasten off.

GRANNY SQUARE
Join first color with sl st to 3rd dc from end of Petal A.

RND 3 (RS): BPsc around same dc, *ch 5, BPsc around 3rd dc on next petal; rep from * around, ending last rep with ch 5, sl st to first sc, fasten off, do not turn. (8 ch-5 sps)

RND 4: Join second color with sl st to next ch-5 sp, 2 sc in same ch-5 sp, *(3 dc, ch 2, 3 dc) in next ch-5 sp, 6 sc in next ch-5 sp; rep from * twice more, (3 dc, ch 2, 3 dc) in next ch-5 sp, 4 sc in first ch-5 sp, sl st to first sc, do not turn. (4 corners, 24 sc)

RND 5: Ch 1, sc in first sc, *skip 1 sc, dc in each of next 3 dc, (2 dc, ch 2, 2 dc) in next ch-2 sp, dc in next 3 dc, skip 1 sc, sc in next sc**, ch 4, skip 2 sc, sc in next sc; rep from * around ending last rep at **, ch 2, join with hdc in first sc, do not turn. (40 dc)

RND 6: Ch 1, sc around post of hdc, *ch 3, skip sc and dc, dc in next 4 dc, (2 dc, ch 2, 2 dc) in next ch-2 sp, dc in next 4 dc**, skip dc and sc, ch 3, sc in next ch-4 sp; rep from * around ending last rep at **, ch 1, join with hdc in first sc, do not turn. (48 dc)

RND 7: Ch 1, sc around post of hdc, *ch 4, sc in ch-3 sp, skip 1 dc, dc in next 5 dc, (2 dc, ch 2, 2 dc) in next ch-2 sp, dc in next 5 dc**, skip 1 dc, sc in next ch-3 sp; rep from * around ending last rep at **, join with sl st to first sc, fasten off, do not turn. (56 dc)

RND 8: Join color F to ch-4 sp, ch 2 (counts as hdc), 3 hdc in same ch-4 sp, *hdc in next 7 dc, 4 hdc in ch-2 sp, hdc in next 7 dc**, 4 hdc in next ch-4 sp; rep from * around ending last rep at **, join with sl st to top of tch, fasten off, weave in ends.

Spiral Motif (Rnds 1 & 2)
Granny Square (Rnds 3–8)

Chart Key

⬯ = chain (ch)

• = slip st (sl st)

+ = single crochet (sc)

T = half double crochet (hdc)

┤ = double crochet (dc)

⌐ = back post single crochet (BPsc)

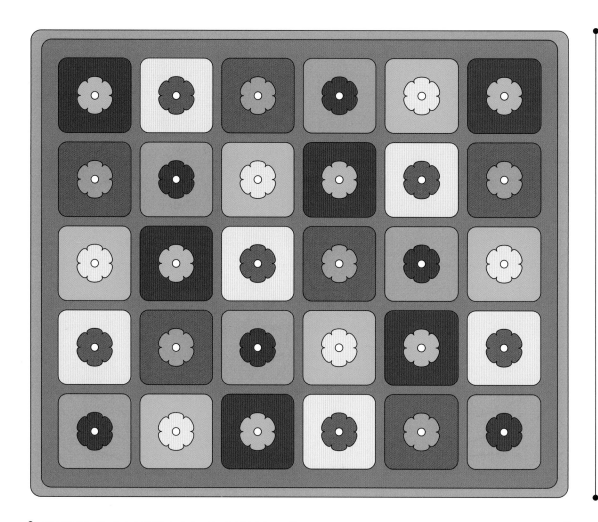

33" (84 cm)

39" (99 cm)

Color Key

- ☐ Dogwood (A)
- ■ Clay (B)
- ■ Frank's Plum (C)
- ■ Split Pea (D)
- ■ Gingerbread (E)
- ■ Storm (F)

FINISHING

Following Motif Layout Diagram, pin two adjoining motifs together with WS facing. Join F to edge of motif with sl st in corner. Sc across both motifs at the same time by crocheting in the front loop of the motif closest to you and the back loop of the one farthest from you. *Tip:* At the end of the motif, have the next 2 motifs pinned and ready to go, then you can keep crocheting across them without having to fasten off and rejoin color F. Cont joining all motifs together.

Join F to RS edge of blanket in a back loop only (blo) with sl st.

RND 1: Ch 2 (counts as hdc), *hdc blo in each st around to 2 hdc of corner, skip first corner hdc, 3 hdc blo in next corner hdc; rep from * around for rem sides and corners, join with sl st to top of beg tch, do not turn.

COLOR TIP

Use this pattern as a
jumping-off point for any
color combination. It would
look gorgeous in shades of
tan, beige, and off-white, for
either a boy or a girl.

RNDS 2 AND 3: Ch 2 (counts as hdc), *hdc in each hdc acround to 3 hdc of corner, hdc in next hdc, 3 hdc in next hdc for corner, hdc in next hdc; rep from * around for rem sides and corners, join with sl st to top of beg tch, do not turn, fasten off.

RND 4: Join B in blo of any st, ch 1,* sc blo in each hdc to corner 3 hdc, 2 sc blo in each of next 3 hdc; rep from * around for rem sides and corners, join with sl st to first sc, fasten off, weave in ends.

Pin blanket to measurements, spray with water, and allow to dry.

pinwheel baby blanket

tissue box cozy

SIZE
To fit 4¼" wide (10.5 cm) × 5" long (12.5 cm) × 4¼" deep (10.5 cm) tissue box.

YARN
Bulky weight (#6 Super Bulky).

Shown here: Rowan Big Wool (100% Merino wool, 87 yd [80 m]/3.5 oz [100 g]), in #55 Eternal (MC), #48 Linen (A), #64 Prize (B), 1 skein each.

HOOK
Size L-11 (8 mm), or size needed to obtain gauge.

NOTIONS
Tapestry needle.

GAUGE
5 sc and 6½ rows = 2" (5 cm) in sc stitch. *Take time to check your gauge.*

Even if you are felled by a cold, you don't have to suffer unsightly tissue boxes. Add a quick crafty touch to your room with this easy tissue box cover, and hide that eyesore of a box once and for all!

DESIGNED BY FAITH HALE

STITCH GUIDE

Sc2tog
(single crochet two together)

Insert hook in next stitch, yarn over and pull up loop (2 loops on hook), insert hook in next stitch, yarn over and pull up loop (3 loops on hook), yarn over and draw through all 3 loops on hook—1 stitch decreased.

Sc3tog
(single crochet three together)

[Insert hook in next stitch, yarn over, pull loop through stitch] 3 times (4 loops on hook). Yarn over and draw yarn through all 4 loops on hook—2 stitches decreased.

NOTE

❖ When changing colors, work the last stitch with working yarn until only one step remains to complete it (e.g., for single crochet, insert hook in next stitch and pull up a loop. Drop working yarn and let it fall to the back of work, yarn over with new yarn and draw through remaining loops on hook to complete stitch. Carry unused color up along WS and continue with new yarn.

COLOR STRATEGY: THE COLOR WHEEL

If you're not using the color wheel when planning your crochet projects, you're missing out on a valuable and easy-to-use tool. The color wheel is a classic tool that has been used by designers and artists for ages, as it is a no-fail way to select complementary colors. Next time you're picking out yarn for a project, visualize the color wheel and try one of these approaches:

✤ Choose two colors that are directly opposite each other on the wheel.

✤ Choose three colors that form a triangle on the wheel.

✤ Choose two colors that are next to or near each other on the wheel.

COZY

SIDE PANEL

With color MC, ch 41, join with sl st to first ch.

RND 1: Sc in 2nd ch and in each ch around—40 sc, do not turn.

RNDS 2–5: Ch 1, sc in first and each sc around, joining color A at end of last rnd, do not turn.

RND 6: With color A, sc in each sc around, joining color MC at end of rnd, do not turn.

RNDS 7 AND 8: With color MC, sc in each sc around joining color B at end of rnd, do not turn.

RND 9: With color B, sc in each sc around, joining color MC at end of rnd, do not turn.

RNDS 10 AND 11: With color MC, sc in each sc around, joining color A at end of rnd, do not turn.

RND 12: With color A, sc in each sc around, joining color MC at end of rnd, do not turn.

RNDS 13–15: With color MC, sc in each sc around, do not fasten off.

TOP

RND 16:]Working in blo, sl st in next 4 back loops, ch 1, sc in first and in each of next 4 sc, *sc2tog (for corner), sc in each of next 8 sc; rep from * twice more, sc2tog, sc in last 3 sc—36 sc, join with sl st in first sc, do not turn.

RND 17: Ch 1, sc in first and in each sc around, do not turn.

RND 18: Ch 1, sc in first and in each of next 3 sc, *sc3tog (for corner), sc in each of next 6 sc; rep from * twice more, sc3tog, sc in last 2 sc—28 sc, join with sl st in first sc, do not turn.

RND 19: Rep Rnd 17.

RND 20: Ch 1, sc in first and in each of next 2 sc, *sc3tog (for corner), sc in each of next 4 sc; rep from * twice more, sc3tog, sc in last sc—20 sc, join with sl st in first sc, fasten off.

FINISHING

Weave in ends.

chevron bedspread

SIZE
54" (137 cm) × 80" (203 cm).

YARN
Worsted weight (#4 Medium).

Shown here: Berroco Comfort (50% superfine nylon/50% superfine acrylic, 210 yd [193 m]/3.5 oz [100 g]), in #9767 Marum (A), #9701 Ivory (B), #9716 Chambray (C), 3 skeins each; #9766 Sable (D), #9761 Lovage (E), #9744 Teal (F), #9769 Petunia (G), 2 skeins each; #9780 Dried Plum (H), #9747 Cadet (I), #9763 Navy Blue (J), #9720 Hummus (K), #9757 Lillet (L), 1 skein each.

HOOK
Size J/10 (6 mm), or size needed to obtain gauge.

NOTIONS
Tapestry needle.

GAUGE
7 ¼ sts and 7 rows = 2" (5 cm) in chevron patt. *Take time to check your gauge.*

Zigzags are back in a big way, and that's great news for crocheters! Jump on the chevron trend with this bed-sized blanket stitched in a soothing woodland palette.

DESIGNED BY KATHIE ENG

NOTES

❖ When changing color, always join new color beg in first ch-1 sp of right side row by drawing up a loop in ch-1 sp and ch 1.

❖ Stripe Color Sequence:

12 rows Marum (A)

5 rows Sable (D)

7 rows Ivory (B)

3 rows Lovage (E)

4 rows Lillet (L)

3 rows Cadet (I)

7 rows Teal (F)

2 rows Navy Blue (J)

12 rows Chambray (C)

5 rows Petunia (G)

2 rows Hummus (K)

7 rows Sable (D)

2 rows Hummus (K)

5 rows Marum (A)

6 rows Dried Plum (H)

2 rows Cadet (I)

4 rows Lovage (E)

3 rows Navy Blue (J)

6 rows Ivory (B)

2 rows Teal (F)

12 rows Chambray (C)

Reverse colors beginning with Teal and working back to Marum.

bedspread

Beg in stripe color sequence with color A, ch 282.

ROW 1 (RS): *Working in back loops of foundation ch,* sc in 2nd ch from hook, [ch 1, skip 1 ch, sc in next ch] 7 times, ch 1, skip 1 ch, (sc, ch 2, sc) in next ch, *[ch 1, skip 1 ch, sc in next ch] 7 times, skip next 2 chs, sc in next ch, [ch 1, skip 1 ch, sc in next ch] 6 times, ch 1, skip 1 ch, (sc, ch 2, sc) in next ch; rep from * across ending with [ch 1, skip 1 ch, sc in next ch] 8 times, ch 1, turn.

ROW 2: Skip first sc, sc in next ch-1 sp, [ch 1, skip next sc, sc in next ch-1 sp] 7 times, ch 1, skip next sc, (sc, ch 2, sc) in next ch-2 sp, * [ch 1, skip next sc, sc in next ch-1 sp] 7 times, skip next 2 sc, sc in next ch-1 sp, [ch 1, skip next sc, sc in next ch-1 sp] 6 times, ch 1, skip next sc, (sc, ch 2, sc) in next ch-2 sp; rep from * across ending with [ch 1, skip next sc, sc in next ch-1 sp] 8 times, ch 1, turn.

ROWS 3–12: Rep Row 2, fasten off color A.

ROW 13 (RS): Join color B as noted above and rep Row 2.

Cont to work rem rows in established chevron patt, completing stripe sequence indicated above, fasten off in last row.

finishing

BORDER

With RS facing, join color G, at bottom corner of fnd ch at right-hand edge, draw up a loop through 2 loops. Beg edging from bottom, up along side as foll:

RND 1 (RS)—RIGHT SIDE EDGE: Ch 3, sl st in same ch, *ch 3, skip 1 row, sl st in end of next row; rep from * across to top ending at next-to-last row, ch 3, skip next-to-last row, (sl st, ch 3, sl st) in corner sc at end of last row, rotate work 90 degrees right, to work along top edge.

RND 1 (RS)—TOP EDGE: Ch 2, sl st in next ch-1 sp, [ch 2, skip next sc, sl st in next ch-1 sp] 7 times, ch 2, skip next sc, (sl st, ch 3, sl st) in next ch-2 sp, *[ch 2, skip next sc, sl st in next ch-1 sp] 7 times, ch 1, skip 2 sc, sl st in next ch-1 sp, [ch 2, skip next sc, sl st in next ch-1 sp] 6 times, ch 2, skip next sc, (sl st, ch 3, sl st) in next ch-2 sp; rep from * along top edge, ending last rep with [ch 2, skip next sc, sl st in next ch-1 sp] 8 times, rotate work 90 degrees to work along side edge.

RND 1 (RS)—LEFT SIDE EDGE: Ch 2, (sl st, ch 3, sl st) in last sc, *ch 3, skip 1 row, sl st in end of next row; rep from * along side edge to next-to-last row, ch 3, skip next row, (sl st, ch 3, sl st) through 2 loops of bottom corner ch, rotate work 90 degrees to work along bottom edge.

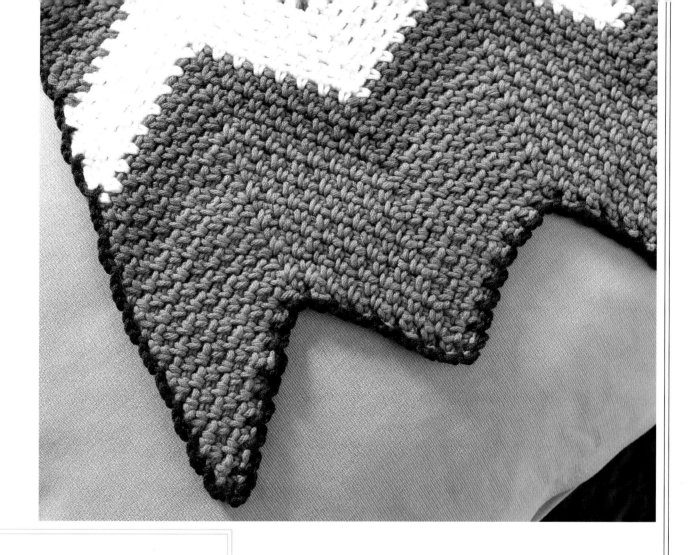

COLOR TIP

One way to plan harmonious color placement is to use symmetry. In this blanket, the stripes are arranged in a mirror image sequence from the center out, a great technique for helping many-hued projects to look less busy.

RND 1 (RS)—BOTTOM EDGE: [Ch 2, skip next ch, sl st in next ch-1 sp] 8 times, *ch 2, skip next ch, sl st in next ch-1 sp, [ch 2, skip next ch, sl st in next ch-1 sp] 6 times, ch 2, skip next ch, (sl st, ch 3, sl st) in next ch-2 sp, [ch 2, skip next ch, sl st in next ch-1 sp] 7 times; rep from * along bottom edge, ending last with [ch 2, skip next ch, sl st in next ch-1 sp] 7 times, ch 2, skip next ch, sl st in beg sl st. Fasten off. Weave in ends to WS.

stitch sampler bolster

SIZE
30" (76 cm) long and 8" (20.5 cm) in diameter.

YARN
DK weight (#3 Light)

Shown here: Cascade Yarns 220 Sport (100% Peruvian Highland wool; 164 yd [150 m]/1.75 oz [50 g]), in #9591 Buff (MC), 3 skeins; #9594 Orchid Haze (A), #9325 Westpoint Blue Heather (B), #8622 Caramel (C), #9430 Highland Green (D), 1 skein each.

HOOK
Size F/5 (3.75 mm), or size needed to obtain gauge.

NOTIONS
Bolster pillow form, 30" × 8" (76 × 20.5 cm); tapestry needle; marking pins.

GAUGE
Center panel: 21 sts and 12 rows = 4" (10 cm) in stitch patt.

Side panels: 18 sts and 18 rows = 4" (10 cm) in overlay stitch patt.

Stretch your stitches to the limit with this big-scale bolster! Heavily textured stitches are combined with soothing stripes for a result that's big on interest but understated in appearance.

DESIGNED BY KATHY MERRICK

STITCH GUIDE
Tr Treble crochet

NOTES
❖ Center panel is worked first, side panels are worked from edges of center panel, then end circles are made separately and sewn on.

❖ When working panel and end circles, do not fasten off MC. Carry MC up as you work until needed again.

bolster

BODY CENTER PANEL
COLOR STRIPE SEQUENCE: [2A, 2MC, 2B, 2MC, 2C, 2MC, 2D, 2MC] 3 times, 2A, 2MC, 2B, 2MC.

Ch 51 with MC.

SET-UP ROW 1: Sc in 2nd ch from hook, *ch 2, skip 2 ch, sc in next 2 ch, ch 2, skip 2 ch, sc in next ch; rep from * across ch 1, turn.

SET-UP ROW 2: Sc in first sc, *ch 2, sc in next 2 sc, ch 2, sc in next sc; rep from * across, do not fasten off MC, change to A and beg color stripe sequence, ch 1, turn.

ROW 1 (RS): With A, sc in first sc, sc in ch-2 sp, *ch 7, sc in 4th ch from hook, hdc in 5th ch, dc in 6th ch, tr in 7th ch, sc in next ch-2 sp, sc in next 2 sc; rep from *, ending last rep with sc in last ch-2 sp, sc in last sc, ch 7, turn.

ROW 2: With A, sc in first sc, *ch 4, 2 sc in ch-3 sp of first group, ch 4, (sc, ch 7, sc) in center sc of 3-sc bet groups; rep from *, ending last rep with (sc, ch 4, tr) tr in last sc, fasten off A, change to MC, ch 1, turn.

ROW 3: With MC, 2 sc in first tr, *ch 2, sc in next 2 sc, ch 2, sc in ch-7 sp; rep from * across, ch 1, turn.

ROW 4: With MC, sc in first sc, *ch 2, sc in next 2 sc, ch 2, sc in next sc; rep from * across, do not fasten off MC, change to B and beg color stripe sequence, ch 1, turn.

ROWS 5-16: Rep Rows 1–4, completing stripe color sequence.

Working in patt as established alternating colors A, B, C, and D, rep stripe color sequence 3 times more, then with colors A and B once more ending with 2MC, fasten off.

BODY CENTER—SIDE PANEL 1
COLOR STRIPE SEQUENCE: [2MC, 2A, 2MC, 2B, 2MC, 2C, 2MC, 2D] 3 times.

With RS facing and MC, beg color stripe sequence, work 93 sc evenly across side of center panel, ch 1, turn.

SET-UP ROW (WS): With MC, sc in first and 2nd sc, *ch 7, skip 4 sc, sc in next 3 sc; rep from * across, ending last rep with sc in last 2 sc, do not fasten off MC, change to A, ch 1, turn.

ROW 1 (RS): With A, sc in first and 2nd sc, *working in back of ch-7 loop of prev row, tr in 4 skipped sc, skip ch-7 sp, sc in 3 sc; rep from *, ending last rep with sc in last 2 sc, ch 1, turn.

ROW 2 (WS): With A, sc in each st across, fasten off A, change to MC, ch 3 (counts as first dc of next row), turn.

ROW 3 (RS): With MC, dc in next sc, *ch 3, sc in ch-7 loop of row 1, ch 3, skip 4 sc behind ch-7 loop , dc in 3 sc; rep from *, ending last rep with dc in last 2 dc, ch 1, turn.

Color Key

■ Buff (MC)

▦ Orchid Haze (A)

▦ Westpoint Blue Heather (B)

▦ Caramel (C)

▦ Highland Green (D)

Chart Key

⬯ = chain (ch)

● = slip st (sl st)

+ = single crochet (sc)

T = half double crochet (hdc)

† = double crochet (dc)

‡ = treble crochet (tr)

⋊⋉ = 2 sc in same st

⏝ = front loop

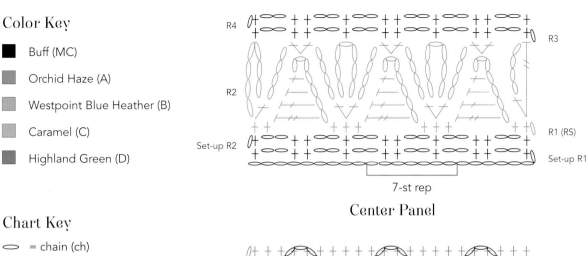

Center Panel

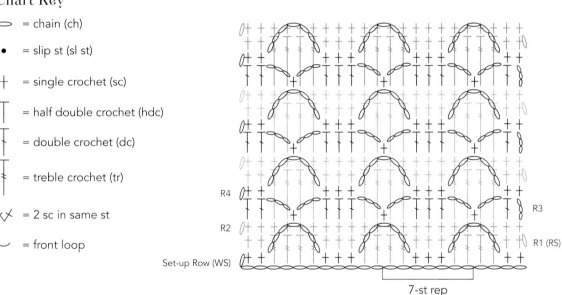

Side Panel Overlay

ROW 4 (WS): With MC, sc in first and 2nd dc, *ch 7, skip 4 sc in row 3, sc in next 3 dc; rep from * across, ending last rep with sc in next dc, sc in top of tch, do not fasten off MC, change to B, ch 1, turn.

Rep Rows 1–4 for patt and cont in color stripe sequence alternating colors A, B, C, and D in Rows 1 and 2, fasten off.

Rep as for Body Side Panel 1.

END PANELS

(Make 2.)

With MC, ch 4, join to first ch to form ring.

RND 1: Ch 3 (counts as dc throughout), 9 dc in ring—10 dc. Join with sl st in top of beg ch-3, do not fasten off MC, join A, do not turn.

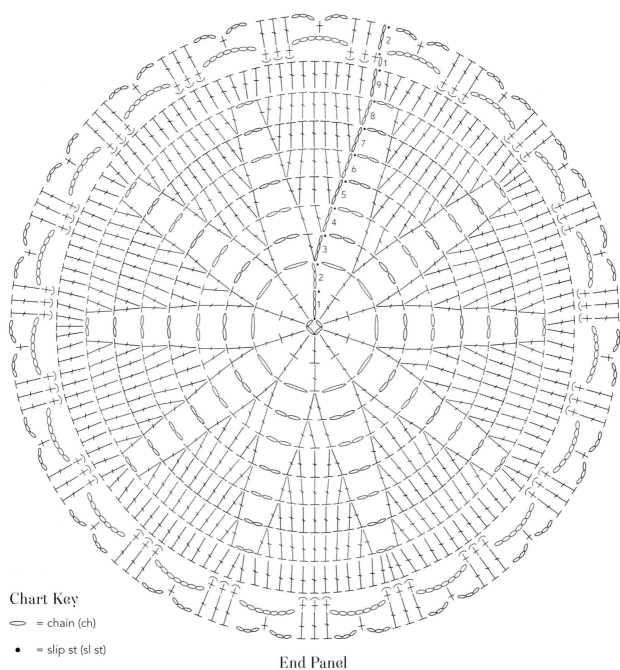

End Panel

Chart Key

◯ = chain (ch)

• = slip st (sl st)

+ = single crochet (sc)

T = half double crochet (hdc)

† = double crochet (dc)

‡ = treble crochet (tr)

⋉⋊ = 2 sc in same st

⌣ = front loop

RND 2: With A, ch 4 (counts as first dc and ch 1), *dc in next dc, ch 1; rep from * around—10 dc and 10 ch-1 sps, join with sl st in 3rd ch of beg ch-4, fasten off A, join MC, do not turn.

RND 3: With MC, ch 3, dc in same sp as joining, ch 2, *2 dc in next dc, ch 2; rep from *, around, join with sl st in top of beg ch-3—20 dc and 10 ch-2 sps, do not fasten off MC, join B, do not turn.

Color Key

- ■ Buff (MC)
- ▨ Orchid Haze (A)
- ▨ Westpoint Blue Heather (B)
- ▨ Caramel (C)
- ▨ Highland Green (D)

RND 4: With B, ch 3, dc in same sp as joining, dc in next dc, ch 2, *2 dc in next dc, dc in next dc, ch 2; rep from * around, join with sl st in top of beg ch-3—30 dc and 10 ch-2 sps, fasten off B, join MC, do not turn.

RND 5: With MC, ch 3, dc in same sp as joining, dc in next dc, 2 dc in next dc, ch 2, *2 dc in next dc, dc in next 2 dc, 2 dc in next dc, ch 2; rep from * around—50 dc and 10 ch-2 sps, join with sl st in top of beg ch-3, do not fasten off MC, join C, do not turn.

RND 6: With C, ch 3, dc in same sp as joining, dc in next 3 dc, 2 dc in next dc, ch 2, *2 dc in next dc, dc in next 3 dc, 2 dc in next dc, ch 2; rep from * around—70 dc and 10 ch-2 sps, join with sl st in top of beg ch-3, fasten off C, join MC, do not turn.

RND 7: With MC, ch 3, dc in same sp as joining, dc in next 5 dc, 2 dc in next dc, ch 2, *2 dc in next dc, dc in next 5 dc, 2 dc in next dc, ch 2, rep from * around—90 dc and 10 ch-2 sps, join with sl st in top of beg ch-3, do not fasten off MC, join D, do not turn.

RND 8: With D, ch 3, dc in same sp as joining, dc in next 7 dc, 2 dc in next dc, ch 2, *2 dc in next dc, dc in next 7 dc, 2 dc in next dc, ch 2; rep from * around—110 dc and 10 ch-2 sps, join with sl st in top of beg ch-3, fasten off D, join MC, do not turn.

RND 9: With MC, ch 3, *[dc in each dc, 2 dc in ch-2 sp] twice, dc in each dc, 3 dc in ch-2 sp; rep from * twice more, dc in each dc, 2 dc in last ch-2 sp—133 dc, join with sl st in top of beg ch-3, do not fasten off MC, do not turn.

edging

RND 1: With MC, working through front loops only, ch 1, sc in first and next 2 sc, *ch 7, skip 4 dc, sc in next 3 sc; rep from * around, ending last rep with ch 7, skip 4 dc, join with sl st to first sc—57 sc and 19 ch-7 sps, do not turn.

RND 2: Ch 3, dc in next 2 dc, *ch 3, sc in ch-7 sp, ch 3, dc in next 3 dc; rep from * around, ending last rep with ch 3, sc in ch-7 sp, ch 3, join with sl st in top of beg ch-3—57 dc and 19 sc. Fasten off.

finishing

Gently steam all pieces to measurements.

With RS tog of center side panels, sl st edges tog with MC, leaving center section open. Pin end panels to each end of side panel, WS tog matching edges, sew tog through back loops of circles. Insert pillow form. Sew edges of center panel closed.

colorful
kitschy
kitchen

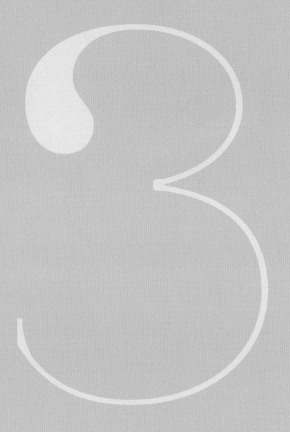

nested squares dishcloths

SIZE
8¾" long × 8" wide
(22 × 20.5 cm).

YARN
Worsted weight (#4 Medium).

Shown here: Peaches & Creme Solids (100% cotton; 120 yd [109 m]/2.5 oz [70.9 g]), in #1628 Bright Orange (A), #1712 Bright Lime (B), #1730 Bright Aqua (C), 2 skeins each.

HOOK
Size J/10 (6 mm), or size needed to obtain gauge.

NOTIONS
Tapestry needle.

GAUGE
Rnds 1–5 = 3¼" (8.5 cm).

Simple single crochet and a snappy color selection make these classic cloths fresh and new. Think outside the box and change yarn whenever you like to create your own color combinations!

DESIGNED BY ELLEN GORMLEY

STITCH GUIDE

Color Block 1:

RNDS 1 AND 2: Color A.

RND 3: Color C.

RNDS 4-13: Color B.

CONTRAST STRIPE: Color C.

EDGING: Color A.

Color Block 2:

RNDS 1-5: Color B.

RND 6: Color A.

RNDS 7-13: Color C.

CONTRAST STRIPE: Color A.

EDGING: Color B.

Color Block 3:

RNDS 1-4: Color C.

RND 5: Color B.

RND 6: Color A.

RND 7: Color B.

RNDS 8-13: Color A.

CONTRAST STRIPE: Color B.

EDGING: Color C.

NOTE

❖ Work rounds for blocks in colors indicated, following instructions for block pattern.

dishcloths

(Make 1 of each block.)

BLOCK PATTERN

Ch 5, join with sl st in first ch.

RND 1 (RS): Ch 1, 8 sc in ring, join with sl st in first sc, turn—8 sc.

RND 2 (WS): Ch 2, (counts as middle dc in corner), sc in same st, *sc in next st, (sc, dc, sc) in next st; rep from * twice more, sc in next st, sc in same st as beg ch-2, join with sl st in top beg ch-2, turn—4 dc, 12 sc.

RND 3: Ch 2, sc in same st, *sc in next 3 sts, (sc, dc, sc) in next dc; rep from * twice more, sc in next 3 sts, sc in same st as the beginning ch-2, join with sl st in top beg ch-2, turn—4 dc, 20 sc.

RND 4: Ch 2, sc in same st, *sc in next 5 sts, (sc, dc, sc) in next dc; rep from * twice more, sc in next 5 sts, sc in same st as the beginning ch-2, join with sl st in top beg ch-2, turn—4 dc, 28 sc.

RND 5: Ch 2, sc in same st, *sc in next 7 sts, (sc, dc, sc) in next dc; rep from * twice more, sc in next 7 sts, sc in same st as the beginning ch-2, join with sl st in top beg ch-2, turn—4 dc, 36 sc.

RND 6: Ch 2, sc in same st, *sc in next 9 sts, (sc, dc, sc) in next dc; rep from * twice more, sc in next 9 sts, sc in same st as the beginning ch-2, join with sl st in top beg ch-2, turn—4 dc, 44 sc.

RND 7: Ch 2, sc in same st, *sc in next 11 sts, (sc, dc, sc) in next dc; rep from * twice more, sc in next 11 sts, sc in same st as the beginning ch-2, join with sl st in top beg ch-2, turn—4 dc, 52 sc.

RND 8: Ch 2, sc in same st, *sc in next 13 sts, (sc, dc, sc) in next dc; rep from * twice more, sc in next 13 sts, sc in same st as the beginning ch-2, join with sl st in top beg ch-2, turn—4 dc, 60 sc.

RND 9: Ch 2, sc in same st, *sc in next 15 sts, (sc, dc, sc) in next dc; rep from * twice more, sc in next 15 sts, sc in same st as the beginning ch-2, join with sl st in top beg ch-2, turn—4 dc, 68 sc.

RND 10: Ch 2, sc in same st, *sc in next 17 sts, (sc, dc, sc) in next dc; rep from * twice more, sc in next 17 sts, sc in same st as the beginning ch-2, join with sl st in top beg ch-2, turn—4 dc, 76 sc.

RND 11: Ch 2, sc in same st, *sc in next 19 sts, (sc, dc, sc) in next dc; rep from * twice more, sc in next 19 sts, sc in same st as the beginning ch-2, join with sl st in top beg ch-2, turn—4 dc, 84 sc.

RND 12: Ch 2, sc in same st, *sc in next 21 sts, (sc, dc, sc) in next dc; rep from * twice more, sc in next 21 sts, sc in same st as the beginning ch-2, join with sl st in top beg ch-2, turn—4 dc, 92 sc.

RND 13: Ch 2, sc in same st, *sc in next 23 sts, (sc, dc, sc) in next dc; rep from * twice more, sc in next 23 sts, sc in same st as the beginning ch-2, join with sl st in top beg ch-2, turn—4 dc, 100 sc. Fasten off.

CONTRAST STRIPE

With RS facing, join new yarn with sc in any dc of a corner, sc in each st to next corner—25 sc. Fasten off.

Chart Key

⬯ = chain (ch)

• = slip st (sl st)

╂ = single crochet (sc)

╤ = double crochet (dc)

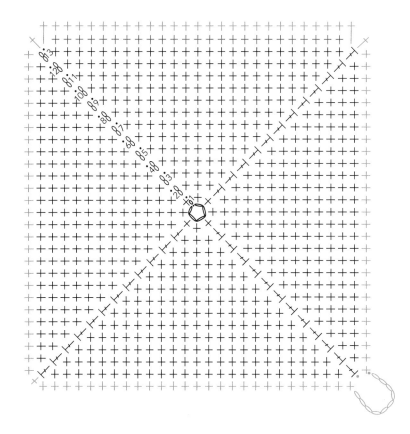

COLOR TIP

The beauty of this design is that you can create a million variations just by switching yarn. Try working a different color on every round for a skinny box-within-a-box effect.

EDGING AND HANGING LOOP

Note: Skip side of sc in contrast stripe when working edging.

With RS facing, join edge color with sc in a dc of the corner diagonal from where the contrast stripe fastened off, *sc in each st to corner, (3 sc) in next corner dc; rep from * twice more, sc in each st to beginning of rnd, sc in same st as first st of rnd, ch 10, join with sl st in first sc. Fasten off.

FINISHING

Weave in ends. Wet block to measurements.

blooming pot holders

SIZE
7" (17.5 cm) in diameter.

YARN
Worsted weight (#4 Medium).

Shown here: Tahki Cotton Classic (100% mercerized cotton; 108 yd [100m]/1.75 oz [50 g]), in #3534 Pale Yellow (A), #3533 Bright Yellow (B), #3549 Gold (C), #3541 Light Cantaloupe (D); Teals: #3777 Aqua (E), #3800 Dark Aqua (F), #3783 Bright Teal (G), #3786 Dark Teal (H); Pinks: #3454 Light Watermelon (I), #3457 Light Raspberry (J), #3461 Light Plum (K), #3456 Bright Raspberry (L), 1 ball each.

HOOK
Size E/4 (3.5 mm), or size needed to obtain gauge.

NOTIONS
Tapestry needle.

GAUGE
4 rnds = 2½" in diameter in dc st. *Take time to check your gauge.*

Outrageous rounds of ruffles take the classic cotton pot holder to a whole new level in this gorgeous design. Stitch up a bunch and give them as gifts to all your favorite cooks.

DESIGNED BY MARYSE ROUDIER

STITCH GUIDE

Color Sequences

Teal Pot Holder (Front and Back)
SET-UP RND AND RND 1: Color D.

RNDS 2 AND 3: Color E.

RNDS 4 AND 5: Color G.

RNDS 6 AND 7: Color H.

RNDS 8 AND 9*: Color F.

Note: Omit Rnd 9 for back.

Pink Pot Holder (Front and Back)
SET-UP RND AND RND 1: Color C.

RNDS 2 AND 3: Color L.

RNDS 4 AND 5: Color I.

RNDS 6 AND 7: Color J.

RNDS 8 AND 9*: Color K.

Note: Omit Rnd 9 for back.

Multicolored Pot Holder (Front)
SET-UP RND AND RND 1: Color B.

RND 2: Color J.

RND 3: Color E.

RND 4: Color A.

RND 5: Color L.

RND 6: Color G.

RND 7: Color C.

RND 8: Color I.

RND 9: Color H.

Multicolored Pot Holder (Back)
SET UP RND, AND RNDS 1 AND 2: Color B.

RNDS 3–5: Color E.

RNDS 6–8: Color I.

NOTES

❖ Yarn amount is enough to make 3 or more pot holders.

❖ Work rounds for each pot holder in colors indicated following instructions for pattern.

❖ When changing color, work to end of round, join with sl st in first stitch of round with new color, then continue work in next round with new color.

pot holder

FRONT

Make an adjustable ring.

SET-UP RND (RS): Ch 1 (counts as sc throughout), 8 sc in ring, join with sl st in beg ch-1, do not turn—9 sc.

RND 1: Ch 3 (counts as dc throughout), dc in same st, 2 dc in each st around, join with sl st in top of beg ch-3, do not turn—18 dc.

RND 2: *Working in front loops,* ch 1, hdc in same st, (dc, tr, dc) in next st, (hdc, sc) in next st, [(sc, hdc) in next st, (dc, tr, dc) in next st, hdc, sc) in next st] 5 times, *working in back loops,* sl st in first st of Rnd 1, ch 3, dc in same st, dc in next st, [2 dc in next st, dc in next st] 8 times, join with sl st in beg ch-1, do not turn.

RND 3: *Working in front loops,* ch 1, hdc in same st, (dc, tr, dc) in next st, (hdc, sc) in next st, [(sc, hdc) in next st, (dc, tr, dc) in next st, (hdc, sc) in next st] 8 times, *working in back loops,* sl st in first st of Rnd 2, ch 3, dc in same st, dc in next 2 sts, [2 dc in next st, dc in next 2 sts] 9 times, join with sl st in beg ch-1, do not turn.

RND 4: *Working in front loops,* ch 1, hdc in same st, (dc, tr, dc) in next st, (hdc, sc) in next st [(sc, hdc) in next st, (dc, tr, dc) in next st, (hdc, sc) in next st] 11 times, *working in back loops,* sl st in first st of Rnd 3, ch 3, dc in same st, dc in next 3 sts [2 dc in next st, dc in next 3 dc] 8 times, join with sl st in beg ch-1, do not turn.

RND 5: *Working in front loops,* ch 1, hdc in same st, (dc, tr, dc) in next st, (hdc, sc) in next st, [(sc, hdc) in next st, (dc, tr, dc) in next st, (hdc, sc) in next st] 14 times, *working in back loops,* sl st in first st of Rnd 4, ch 3, dc in same st, dc in next 4 sts [2 dc in next st, dc in next 4 dc] 8 times, join with sl st in beg ch-1, do not turn.

RND 6: *Working in front loops,* ch 1, hdc in same st, (dc, tr, dc) in next st, (hdc, sc) in next st, [(sc, hdc) in next st, (dc, tr, dc) in next st, (hdc, sc) in next st] 17 times, *working in back loops,* sl st in first st of Rnd 5, ch 3, dc in same st, dc in next 5 sts, [2 dc in next stitch, dc in next 5 dc] 8 times, join with sl st in beg ch-1, do not turn.

RND 7: *Working in front loops,* ch 1, hdc in same st, (dc, tr, dc) in next st, (hdc, sc) in next st, [(sc, hdc) in next st, (dc, tr, dc) in next st, (hdc, sc) in next st] 20 times, *working in back loops,* sl st in first st of Rnd 6, ch 3, dc in same st, dc in next 6 sts, [2 dc in next stitch, dc in next 6 dc] 8 times, join with sl st in beg ch-1, do not turn.

RND 8: *Working in front loops,* ch 1, hdc in same st, (dc, tr, dc) in next st, (hdc, sc) in next st, [(sc, hdc) in next st, (dc, tr, dc) in next st, (hdc, sc) in next st] 23 times, *working in back loops,* sl st in first st of Rnd 7, ch 3, dc in same st, dc in next 7 sts, [2 dc in next stitch, dc in next 7 dc] 8 times, join with sl st in beg ch-1, do not turn.

RND 9: *Working in front loops,* ch 1, hdc in same st, (dc, tr, dc) in next st, (hdc, sc) in next st, [(sc, hdc) in next st, (dc, tr, dc) in next st, (hdc, sc) in next st] 26 times, join with sl st in beg ch-1, fasten off.

COLOR STRATEGY: ALL IN THE FAMILY

If you're looking for a way to use vibrant color in your projects without going colorful or child-like, try selecting three or more shades of the same color. A group of teals, pinks, oranges or any shade clustered together will give your project depth and life, without going too crazy.

COLOR TIP

Choose a range of four shades of any color for the rounds of these pot holders, for a look that's bold yet not over-the-top. For a crazy colorful effect, choose several contrasting shades.

BACK

Make an adjustable ring.

SET-UPRND (RS): Ch 1 (counts as sc), 8 sc in ring, join with sl st in beg ch-1, do not turn—9 sc.

RND 1: Ch 3 (counts as dc throughout), dc in same st, [2 dc in each sc] 9 times, join with sl st in top of beg ch-3, do not turn—18 dc.

RND 2: Ch 3, dc in same st, dc in next dc, [2 dc in next stitch, dc in next dc] 8 times, join with sl st in top of beg ch-3, do not turn—27 dc.

RND 3: Ch 3, dc in same st, dc in next 2 dc, [2 dc in next st, dc in next 2 dc] 8 times, join with sl st in top of beg ch-3, do not turn—36 dc.

RND 4: Ch 3, dc in same st, dc in next 3 dc, [2 dc in next st, dc in next 3 dc] 8 times, join with sl st in top of beg ch-3, do not turn—45 dc.

RND 5: Ch 3, dc in same st, dc in next 4 dc, [2 dc in next st, dc in next 4 dc] 8 times, join with sl st in top of beg ch-3, do not turn—54 dc.

RND 6: Ch 3, dc in same st, dc in next 5 dc, [2 dc in next st, dc in next 5 dc] 8 times, join with sl st in top of beg ch-3, do not turn—63 dc.

RND 7: Ch 3, dc in same st, dc in next 6 dc, [2 dc in next st, dc in next 6 dc] 8 times, join with sl st in top of beg ch-3, do not turn—72 dc.

RND 8: Ch 3, dc in same st, dc in next 7 dc, [2 dc in next st, dc in next 7 dc] 8 times, join with sl st in top of beg ch-3, do not fasten off—81 dc.

FINISHING

Joining Front to Back
Place wrong sides together.

RND 1: Sl st through both dcs around perimeter, join with sl st in first sl st, do not fasten off.

Hanging Loop
Ch 15, sl st through first st, fasten off. Weave in ends.

watermelon coasters

SIZE
5¼" (13.5 cm) in diameter.

YARN
Worsted weight (#4 Medium).

Shown here: Premier Dream (100% acrylic, 224 yd [205 m]/100g), in #24-217 Meadow (A), #24-216 Baby Fern (B), #24-215 Hot Lime (C), #24-201 White (D), #24-206 Grenadine (E), #24-245 Rouge Red (F), #24-235 Black (G), 1 ball each.

HOOK
Size H/8 (5 mm), or size needed to obtain gauge.

NOTIONS
Tapestry needle.

GAUGE
Rnds 1–3 = 1¾" (4.5 cm) in diameter in sc stitch.

It's summer in the kitchen all year long with these cheery coasters. The yarn required is enough to make many coasters. Stitch these up for quick teacher gifts, favors, or fundraisers.

DESIGNED BY AMY POLCYN

NOTES

❖ There is enough yarn to complete 4 or more coasters; only a small amount is needed for each.

❖ When changing color, work to end of round, join with sl st in first stitch of round with new color, then continue work in next round with new color.

coaster

(Make 4.)

With color F, ch 2.

RND 1 (RS): 7 Sc in 2nd ch from hook, join with sl st in first sc, do not turn—7 sc.

RND 2: Ch 1, work 2 sc in each sc around, join with sl st in first sc, do not turn—14 sc.

RND 3: Ch 1, *sc in sc, 2 sc in next sc; rep from * around, join with sl st in first sc, do not turn—21 sc.

RND 4: Ch 1, *sc in 2 sc, 2 sc in next sc; rep from * around, join with sl st in first sc, do not turn—28 sc. Fasten off F.

RND 5: With E, join with sl st, ch 1, *sc in 3 sc, 2 sc in next sc; rep from * around, join with sl st in first sc, do not turn—35 sc. Fasten off E.

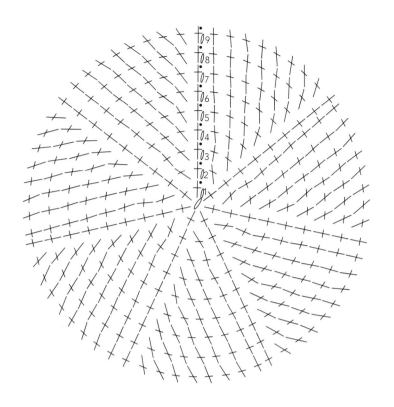

Chart Key

$\bigcirc$ = chain (ch)

• = slip st (sl st)

+ = single crochet (sc)

COLOR TIP

What makes these coasters
watermelon-flavored? The
red centers! Switch them to
yellow or green, and you have
lemons and limes.

RND 6: With D, join with sl st, ch 1, *sc in 4 sc, 2 sc in next sc; rep from
* around, join with sl st in first sc, do not turn—42 sc. Fasten off D.

RND 7: With C, join with sl st, ch 1, *sc in 5 sc, 2 sc in next sc; rep from
* around, join with sl st in first sc, do not turn—49 sc. Fasten off C.

RND 8: With B, join with sl st, ch 1, *sc in 6 sc, 2 sc in next sc; rep from
* around, join with sl st in first sc, do not turn—56 sc. Fasten off B.

RND 9: With A, join with sl st, ch 1, *sc in 7 sc, 2 sc in next sc; rep from
* around, join with sl st in first sc, do not turn—63 sc. Fasten off A.

FINISHING

Weave in ends. Block lightly.

With G, embroider short stitches for seeds around center of coaster
(see photo).

racy pink runner

SIZE
19" (48 cm) × 45" (114 cm) blocked.

For a runner with different dimensions, simply add more squares to the length or width as desired (additional yarn may be required).

YARN
DK weight (#3 Light).

Shown here: Patons Grace (100% mercerized cotton, 136 yd [125 m]/1.75 oz [50 g]), in #62436 Wildberry, 6 skeins (see notes).

HOOK
Size G/6 (4 mm), or size needed to obtain gauge.

NOTIONS
Tapestry needle.

GAUGE
(not critical, see Notes)

2 rnds = 3½" (9 cm) in diameter in motif patt.

1 motif (5 rnds) = 6½" (16.5 cm) in diameter.

The old-fashioned lace table runner gets a modern update in this design thanks to an eye-popping shade of hot pink cotton worked in an exploded gauge. The squares are joined to each other as you go, which makes finishing a breeze.

DESIGNED BY DORIS CHAN

STITCH GUIDE

Motif Pattern

Ch 5, sl st in 5th ch from hook to form a ring, do not turn.

RND 1 (RS): Ch 4 (counts as tr), 2 tr in ring, [ch 6, 3 tr in ring] 3 times, end with ch 3, dc in 4th ch of beg ch (ch 3 and dc counts as ch 6), do not turn—12 tr and 4 ch-6 sps.

RND 2: Ch 4, 5 tr in beg sp, [(6tr, ch 3, 6 tr) in next ch-6 sp] 3 times, 6 tr in same sp as beg, ch 1, hdc in 4th ch of beg ch (ch 1 and hdc counts as ch 3), do not turn—48 tr and 4 ch-3 sps.

RND 3: Ch 1, 2 sc in beg sp, *sc in each of next 4 tr, ch 10, skip next 5 chs from hook, sc in each of next 3 chs, ch 2, skip next 4 tr, sc in each of next 4 tr**, [2 sc, ch 2, 2 sc] in next ch-3 sp*; repeat from * to * twice more, then rep from * to ** once, end with 2 sc in same sp as beg, ch 1, sc in beg sc (ch 1 and sc counts as ch 2), do not turn.

RND 4: Ch 1, sc in beg sp (sc), *sc in each of next 3 sc, ch 4, skip next 3 sc and 3-sc bar, [tr, (ch 4, tr) 3 times] in ch-5 loop at end of bar, ch 4, skip 3 sc of bar and next 3 sc, sc in each of next 3 sc,** (sc, ch 2, sc) in next ch-2 sp*; rep from * to * twice more, then rep from * to ** once, end with sc in same sp as beg, ch 1, sc in beg sc, do not turn.

RND 5: Ch 1, sc in beg sp (sc), *sc in each of next 2 sc, ch 3, skip next 2 sc, sc in next ch-4 sp, skip next tr, [sc, ch 2, 3 dc, ch 2, sc] in next ch-4 sp, skip next tr, [sc, ch 2, 5 dc, ch 2, sc] for corner in next ch-4 sp, skip next tr, [sc, ch 2, 3 dc, ch 2, sc] in next ch-4 sp, skip next tr, sc in next ch- 4 sp, ch 3, skip next 2 sc, sc in each of next 2 sc**, [sc, ch 2, sc] in next ch-2 sp*; repeat from * to * twice more, then rep from * to ** once, end with sc in same sp as beg, ch 2, sl st in beg sc, fasten off.

Connecting Motifs

Motifs are joined to each other along sides, from just past the 5-dc group at the center of a corner to just before the 5-dc group at the center of the next corner.

RNDS 1–4: Complete the working motif through Rnd 4.

With right sides facing, hold working motif below or to the left of the previous motif or motifs already assembled.

RND 5 (CONNECT SIDE): Complete 5 dc of a corner just before the motif side you need to connect, match the next side with the corresponding side of the previous motif, sl st from front to back in the ch-2 sp of the previous motif (just after 5-dc of corner), ch 2, sc in the same ch-4 sp of the working motif, skip next tr, sc in the next ch-4 sp of working motif, ch 2, sl st in next ch-2 sp of previous motif, (3 dc, ch 2, sc) in same ch-4 sp of working motif, skip next tr, sc in next ch-4 sp, ch 3, skip next 2 sc, sc in each of next 2 sc, sc in next ch-2 sp, ch 1, sl st in corresponding ch-2 sp (at center of side between 2 sc) of previous motif, ch 1, sc in same ch-2 sp of working motif, sc in each of next 2 sc, ch 3, skip next 2 sc, sc in next ch-4 sp, skip next tr, [sc, ch 2, 3 dc] in next ch-4 sp, sl st in corresponding ch-2 sp of previous motif (just after next 3 dc), ch 2, sc in same ch-4 sp of working motif, skip next tr, sc in next ch-4 sp, ch 2, sl st in next ch-2 sp of previous motif (just before 5 dc of corner), 5 dc in same ch-4 sp of working motif. Continue to connect another side or complete the motif as indicated.

NOTES

❖ Gauge is a firm but not tight gauge (firmer than for garment fabric), in order to give the table runner some body.

❖ Though gauge is not crucial, if size of runner is larger than finished size, extra yarn may be required to complete all 21 motifs.

runner

Make and assemble 21 motifs in a rectangle, 3 motifs wide by 7 motifs long, connecting motifs to each other as you go while crocheting the last round of each, according to assembly diagram.

Note: You may assemble motifs in any order, but doing it this way allows you to easily adjust the length, in case you change your mind or run out of yarn toward the end.

FIRST COURSE

MOTIF 1: Make one square motif complete.

MOTIF 2: Work Rnd 5 through the 5 dc at the center of corner, connect next side to one side of Motif 1, finish rest of motif.

MOTIF 3: Work Rnd 5 though the 5 dc at center of corner, connect next side to Motif 2, finish rest of motif.

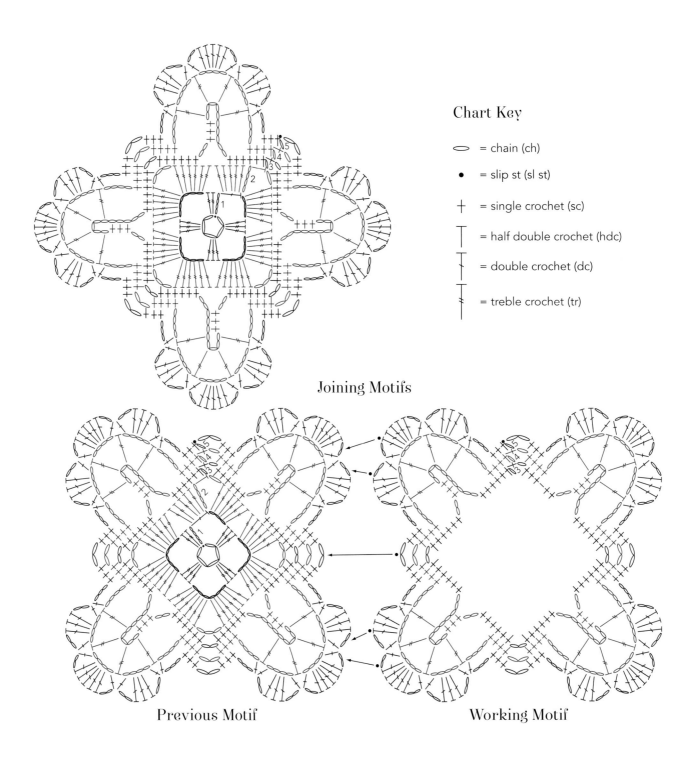

Chart Key

$\bigcirc$ = chain (ch)

• = slip st (sl st)

+ = single crochet (sc)

| = half double crochet (hdc)

† = double crochet (dc)

‡ = treble crochet (tr)

Joining Motifs

Previous Motif

Working Motif

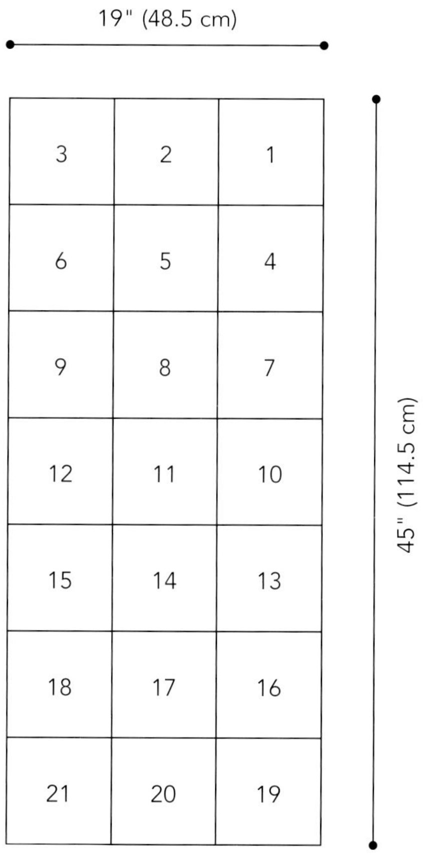

19" (48.5 cm)

3	2	1
6	5	4
9	8	7
12	11	10
15	14	13
18	17	16
21	20	19

45" (114.5 cm)

Table Runner Assembly

SECOND COURSE

MOTIF 4: Work Rnd 5 through the 5 dc at center of a corner, connect next side to Motif 1, finish rest of motif.

MOTIF 5: Work Rnd 5 through the 5 dc at center of a corner, connect next side to Motif 4, connect next side to Motif 2, finish rest of motif.

MOTIF 6: Work Rnd 5 through the 5 dc at center of a corner, connect next side to Motif 5, connect next side to Motif 3, finish rest of motif.

Continue to connect five more courses of 3 motifs in the same way as Second Course.

FINISHING
Weave ends. Block to measurements.

COLOR TIP

The trick to making such a bold color work on your table? Keep everything else simple. Set this hot pink runner on a pale-colored table and choose solid white plates, for a look that allows the crochet to pop without becoming too busy for the eye.

overstuffed seat cushions

SIZE
13" × 16" (33 × 40.5 cm).

YARN
Worsted weight (#4 Medium).

Shown here: Berroco Comfort (50% superfine nylon, 50% superfine acrylic, 210 yd [193 m]/3.5 oz [100 g]), in #9733 Turquoise (A), #9764 Lidfors (B), #9753 Aegean Sea (C), #9725 Dutch Teal (D), 2 skeins each.

HOOK
Size J/10 (6 mm), or size needed to obtain gauge.

NOTIONS
Airtex "regular density" foam chair pad, 1" × 15" × 17" (2.5 × 38 × 43 cm), color white (available at airtex.com); tapestry needle.

GAUGE
Rnds 1–6 = 6" × 7" (15 × 18 cm) in motif patt.

Take your chairs from simple to snazzy with a new set of crocheted seat cushions! In this clever design, ravioli-like cushioned segments add plenty of comfort and a unique take on the basic chair pad.

DESIGNED BY ELLEN GORMLEY

STITCH GUIDE

Standing Single or Double Crochet

Place slipknot on hook and join to motif with the indicated stitch. This replaces joining new yarn with slip stitch and beginning chain.

cushions

COLOR SEQUENCE CHART

TOP	MAT A	MAT B	MAT C	MAT D
Rnd 1	A	B	C	D
Rnd 2	A	B	C	D
Rnd 3	B	D	A	A
Rnd 4	C	A	B	B
Rnd 5	A	B	C	D
Rnd 6	A	B	C	D
BOTTOM				
Rnds 1–6 (Solid)	B	D	A	C
Sl st Rnd	B	D	A	C
Rnd 7 (Border)	B	D	A	C
Join 4 Sections	B	D	A	C
Border	B	D	A	C

PREPARE FOAM

Note: All four seat mats can be made from one piece of 15" × 17" (38 × 43 cm) foam.

Cut 16 foam rectangles, each 4½" × 3" (11.5 × 7.5 cm). Snip and round off all four corners to form rounded rectangle. Four inserts will be used for each seat mat.

MOTIF PATTERN

(For each seat mat, make 4 for top layer and 4 for bottom layer following color sequence chart.)

Ch 8.

RND 1 (RS): 5 dc in 4th ch from hook, (skipped 3 ch count as first dc), dc in next 3 ch, 6 dc in last ch, rotate to work in underside of foundation chs, dc in next 3 ch, join with sl st in top beg ch-3, do not turn—18 dc.

RND 2: Ch 2 (count as first dc throughout) dc in same st, 2 dc in next 5 sts, dc in next 3 sts, 2 dc in each of next 6 sts, dc in last 3 sts; join with sl st in top of beg ch-2, do not turn—30 dc.

RND 3: Ch 2, or join new color with standing dc where previously fastened off, [2 dc in next st, dc in next st] 6 times, dc in next 3 sts, [2 dc in next st, dc in next st] 6 times, dc in last 2 sts, join with sl st in top of beg ch-2, do not turn—42 dc.

RND 4: Ch 2, or join new color with standing dc where previously fastened off, dc in next st, [2 dc in next st, dc in next 2 sts] 6 times, dc in next 3 sts, [2 dc in next st, dc in next 2 sts] 6 times, dc in last st, join with sl st in top of beg ch-2, do not turn—54 dc.

RND 5: Ch 1, sc in same st or join with standing sc, sc in next 4 sts, hdc in next st, 3 dc in next st, hdc in next st, sc in next 8 sts, hdc in next st, 3 dc in next st, hdc in next st, sc in next 13 sts, hdc in next st, 3 dc in next st, hdc in next st, sc in next 8 sts, hdc in next st, 3 dc in next st, hdc in next st, sc in last 8 sts, join with sl st in first sc, do not turn—62 sts (12 dc, 8 hdc, 42 sc).

RND 6: Ch 2, or join with standing dc, dc in next 6 sts, 3 dc in next st, dc in next 12 sts, 3 dc in next st, dc in next 17 sts, 3 dc in next st, dc in next 12 sts, 3 dc in next st, dc in last 10 sts, join with sl st in top of beg ch-2, do not turn—70 dc.

Place WS of top and bottom tog matching shape.

SLIP ST RND: Work surface sl st from top through both layers between Rnds 4 and 5 approx ¾ of the way around leaving opening, insert foam and continue sl st until rnd is complete, join to first sl st.

RND 7: Working through both layers of motifs, join with standing sc in middle dc of any dc-3 corner, 2 sc in same st, *sc in each st across to next corner, 3 sc in middle dc of 3-dc corner; rep from * around ending last rep with sc in each st across to first sc, join with sl st in first st, fasten off—78 sc.

JOINING SEAT MAT SECTIONS
With RS tog of rectangles 1 and 2, join short edge with sc working through the outer loops only. Repeat for rectangles 3 and 4. With RS tog of both rectangles, join long edge with sc working through the outer loops only.

Border
RND 1: Join with standing sc in middle sc of any corner, 2 sc in same st, *sc in each st across to next corner, 3 sc in corner; rep from * ending last rep with sc in each across to first sc, join with sl st in first sc—144 sc.

RND 2: Working in back loops only, ch 2, 3 dc in middle sc of 3-sc corner, *dc in each st across to next corner, 3 dc in middle st of 3-sc corner; rep from * around, ending last rep with dc in each st to first dc, join with slip st in top of beg ch-2—152 dc.

RND 3: Sl st in every st around, fasten off leaving 6" (15 cm) tail—152 sl st.

FINISHING
Weave in end into first sl st in Rnd 3.

COLOR TIP

What makes these cushions pop? They employ the classic color strategy of choosing two shades (blue and yellow) that are directly opposite on the color wheel. For a quieter cushion, use two hues that are neighbors on the wheel.

tiered tea cozy

SIZE
To fit 9" × 6" (23 × 15 cm) teapot.

YARN
Worsted weight (#4 Medium).

Shown here: Quince and Co. Lark (100% American wool, 134 yd [123 m]/1.75 oz [50 g]), in Rosa Rugosta (A), Sorbet (B), Crocus (C), 1 hank each.

HOOK
Size J/10 (6 mm), or size needed to obtain gauge.

NOTIONS
2 stitch markers; porcelain teapot, 9" × 6" (23 × 15 cm), in white.

GAUGE
4 sts and 5 rows = 1" (2.5 cm) in sc stitch.

Deck out your teapot in layers of ruffles that are one part couture gown, one part mad tea party! It has the added bonus of keeping your tea warm.

DESIGNED BY ANA PAULA RIMOLI

NOTES

* ❖ Place marker to indicate beginning of rounds, moving marker up each round while working in spiral.

* ❖ If necessary, place 2nd marker to indicate beginning of rounds when working in front loop, leaving first marker in previous row to indicate first stitch when working in back loop in following row.

* ❖ When changing colors, work the last stitch with working yarn until only one step remains to complete it (e.g., for single crochet, insert hook in next stitch and pull up a loop. Fasten off working yarn leaving 6" (15 cm) tail, yarn over with new yarn and draw through remaining loops on hook to complete stitch. Continue with new yarn.

tea cozy

With yarn A, ch 12 loosely, join with a sl st to form a ring.

RND 1 (RS): Ch 1 (counts as sc), sc in next 11 ch—12 sc.

RND 2: *Working in front loops only,* [4 dc in next st, sl st in next st] 6 times—6 dc groups, 6 sl sts.

RND 3: *Working in back loops only of Rnd 1,* [sc in next sc, 2 sc in next sc] 6 times—18 sc.

RND 4: *Working in front loops only,* [4 dc in next sc, sl st in next sc] 9 times—9 dc groups, 9 sl sts.

RND 5: *Working in back loops only of Rnd 3,* [sc in next 2 sc, 2 sc in next sc] 6 times—24 sc.

RND 6: *Working in front loops only,* [4 dc in next sc, sl st in next sc] 12 times—12 dc groups, 12 sl sts.

RND 7: *Working in back loops only of Rnd 5,* [sc in next 3 sc, 2 sc in next sc] 6 times—30 sc.

RND 8: [Sc in next 4 sc, 2 sc in next sc] 6 times—36 sts. Change to yarn B.

RND 9: Sc in each sc around.

RND 10: [Sc in next 5 sc, 2 sc in next sc] 6 times—42 sc.

RND 11: [Sc in next 6 sc, 2 sc in next sc] 6 times—48 sc.

RND 12: *Working in front loops only,* [4 dc in next sc, sl st in next sc, sc in next sc] 16 times—16 dc groups, 16 sc.

RND 13: *Working in back loops only of Rnd 11,* sc in each sc around—48 sc.

RND 14: [Sc in next 7 sc, 2 sc in next sc] 6 times—54 sc.

RND 15: *Working in front loops only,* [4 dc in next sc, sl st in next sc, sc in next sc] 18 times—18 dc groups, 18 sl sts, 18 sc.

RND 16: *Working in back loops only of Rnd 14,* sc in each sc around.

RND 17: Sc in each sc around.

RND 18: Rep Rnd 15. This is the end of spiral rnds.

Beg working in rows as foll:

Note: For Side 1, beg of rows is the handle opening and end of rows is spout opening.

HANDLE AND SPOUT OPENINGS

ROW 19 (RS): Ch 1, *working in back loops only of Rnd 17,* sc in each sc around, turn—54 sc.

ROW 20: Ch 1, sc in each sc around, turn. Change to yarn C.

ROW 21: *Working in front loops only,* [4 dc in next sc, sl st in next sc, sc in next sc] 18 times, turn—18 dc groups, 18 sl st, 18 sc.

COLOR TIP

It's easy for ruffles to look dated, but choosing three shades of yarn that are all close in tone, and grouping them together in wide bands, makes these ruffles quirky, modern, and sophisticated.

Side 1

ROWS 22 AND 24: Ch 2 (counts as dc), *working in back loops only of Row 20 (22),* dc in next 27 sc, turn—28 dc.

ROWS 23 AND 25: *Working in front loops only,* [4 dc in next dc, sl st in next dc, sc in next dc] 9 times, ending last rep with sl st in last dc, turn.

ROW 26: Ch 2, *working in back loops only of Row 24,* dc in next 27 sc, turn—28 dc. Change to yarn A.

ROWS 27, 29, AND 31: *Working in front loops only,* [4 dc in next dc, sl st in next dc, sc in next dc] 9 times, ending last rep with sl st in last dc, turn.

ROWS 28, 30, AND 32: Ch 2, *working in back loops only of Row 26 (28, 30),* dc in next 27 sc, turn—28 dc. Change to yarn B at end of Row 32.

ROWS 33 AND 35: *Working in front loops only,* [4 dc in next dc, sl st in next dc, sc in next dc] 9 times, ending last rep with sl st in last dc, turn.

ROW 34: Ch 2, *working in back loops only of Row 32,* dc in next 27 sc, turn—28 dc.

ROW 36: Ch 2, *working in back loops only of Row 34,* dc in st decreasing 6 sts evenly across, turn—22 dc.

ROW 37: *Working in front loops only,* [4 dc in next dc, sl st in next dc, sc in next dc] 7 times, ending last rep with sl st in last dc, fasten off.

Side 2

With WS facing, join yarn C to last st worked of Row 21, turn.

Rep Rows 22–37 of Side 1, do not fasten off, turn.

BOTTOM BAND

Ch 1 (counts as sc), *working in back loops only of Side 2,* sc in next 21 sc, ch 7, *working in back loops only,* sc in next 22 sc of Side 1, ch 7 join with sl st in beg ch-1, turn—44 sc, 14 ch.

RND 39: Ch 1 (counts as sc), sc in next 21 sc, sc in next 7 ch, sc in next 22 sc, sc in next 7 ch, join with sl st in beg ch-1—58 sc.

RNDS 40–42: Ch 1 (counts as sc), sc in next 57 sc, join with sl st in beg ch-1, fasten off.

FINISHING

Weave in ends.

Go prepare some tea, and keep it warm with your new little teapot sweater!

flowering trivets

SIZE
8½" × 8½" square
(21.5 × 21.5 cm).

YARN
Worsted weight (#4 Medium).

Shown here: Spud and Chloë
Sweater (Superwash 55%
wool/45% organic cotton,
160 yd [146 m]/3.5 oz [100 g]),
in #7510 Splash (A), #7509
Firecracker (B), #7508 Pollen
(C), #7515 Cider (D), 1 hank
each.

HOOK
Size G/6 (4 mm), or size
needed to obtain gauge.

NOTIONS
Tapestry needle.

GAUGE
One flower motif about
3" (7.5 cm) in diameter.

Chunky, flowerlike motifs are all it takes
to make these simple trivets. They're easy
to customize, too: make and connect more
motifs to create your own table runner,
place mats, and more.

DESIGNED BY REGINA RIOUX

COLOR TIP

Location is everything in this design. Placing the colors in a grid, like our version, is one option. For a totally different look, place your colors in diagonal strips, or try making the outer round of each motif the same color with all the centers in different hues.

trivets

Trivet 1
Make 5 motifs in colors A and B; 4 motifs in colors B and A.

Trivet 2
Make 5 motifs in colors C and D; 4 motifs in colors D and C.

With first color, ch 4.

RND 1 (RS): 11 dc in 4th ch from hook, join with sl st in top of beg ch-3, fasten off first color, do not turn—12 sts.

RND 2: Join second color in any dc, ch 3 (counts as dc), 4 dc in same st as joining, sl st in top of beg ch-3 to close group, ch 2, [5 dc in next st, sl st in top of beg dc to join ch 2] 11 times, join with sl st in top of beg ch-3, fasten off leaving 12" (30.5 cm) tail for sewing motifs together.

FINISHING

Motif Assembly
Lay motifs following diagram. Beginning with top row, sew motifs together on the WS at each side (attaching approx 3 petals per side). Repeat for 2nd and 3rd rows.

To join rows, repeat as for sides attaching 3 petals per motif. Weave in ends.

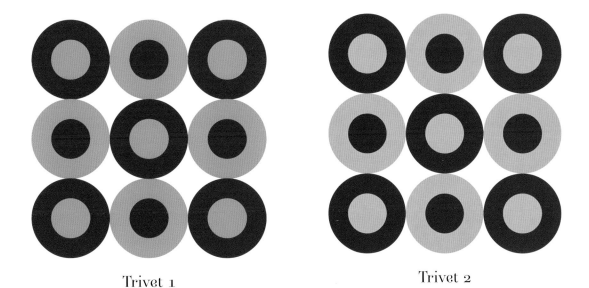

Trivet 1   Trivet 2

Color Key

| | Splash (A) | | Pollen (C) |
| | Firecracker (B) | | Cider (D) |

COLOR STRATEGY: OPPOSITES ATTRACT

If a vibrant kick of color is what you're after, the easiest way to achieve this is to select two shades that are directly opposite each other on the color wheel. Blue and orange, red and green-—these may not be colors that you think of as "matching," but when combined, they are guaranteed to pop in a way that's harmonious and pleasing to the eye.

pinwheel pot scrubbies

SIZE
9" (23 cm) circumference, stuffed.

YARN
DK weight (#3 Light).

Shown here: Cascade Yarns Fixation (98.3% cotton, 1.7% elasticlend, 100 yd [91 m]/1.75 oz [50 g])

Solid: #3794 Wine (A), #5806 Granny Smith Green (A), and #8176 Ecru (C), 2 balls each.

Effects: #9398 Hot Pink (D), 2 balls.

HOOK
Size G/6 (4 mm), or size needed to obtain gauge.

NOTIONS
Polyester stuffing or other synthetic material for stuffing (old nylons or tights work very well!); tapestry needle.

GAUGE
4 sts and 2 rows = 1" (2.5 cm) in dc stitch using 2 strands of yarn. *Take time to check your gauge.*

Doing the dishes just became a lot more fun, thanks to these colorful scrubby orbs. A clever two-tone spiral stitch pattern makes them interesting to crochet, too.

DESIGNED BY CAL PATCH

- Two balls of yarn will make at least 3 or 4 scrubbies.
- Two strands of yarn are used throughout. *Tip:* Use both ends of yarn ball, one from the inside and the other from the outside, at the same time.
- First color (A) and 2nd color (B) are worked alternately to form a spiral.
- When changing colors, do not fasten off but drop yarn to back. Carry up unused color on WS until needed.

scrubbies

Make 1st Half in color combinations, reversing colors in 2nd Half:

A/B, C/D, A/D, B/C, B/D.

1ST HALF

RND 1 (RS): With 2 strands of yarn, ch 3, 6 dc in 3rd ch from hook.

RND 2: Drop color A and make a slipknot in color B; join with sl st in 2nd of original 3 ch, ch 1, (sc, hdc) in next ch st, 2 dc in each of next 6 dc (You are at the last st of color A. Drop B without fastening off and pick up A.)—14 sts.

RND 3: With color A, 2 dc in next ch (the ch-1 of color B), *2 dc in next st, 1 dc in next st, rep from * to end of color B, drop A, pick up B—23 sts.

RND 4: With color B, (dc in next st, 2 dc in next st) 3 times, (dc in next 2 sts, 2 dc in next st) 4 times, hdc in next 2 sts, sc in next 2 sts, sl st in next 2 sts—31 sts, fasten off B, pick up A.

RND 5: With A, dc in next st, 2 dc in next st, (dc in next 2 sts, 2 dc in next st) 2 times, hdc in next 2 sts, sc in next 2 sts, sl st in next 2 sts—17 sts, fasten off.

COLOR TIP

The trick to a cohesive set of scrubbies that aren't matchy-matchy? Choose one or two main colors, then accent with variety. Try working one half of the spiral in black on all the scrubbies, then using a different bright color for the other half of the spiral on each one.

2ND HALF

Repeat as for 1st Half, reversing colors A and B. Do not fasten off.

FINISHING

After completing Rnd 5, place edges tog with 1st Half with WS to inside. Join edges by working slip stitch through both layers around outer edges leaving about 2" (5 cm) opening. Stuff with fiberfill or another synthetic material such as old pantyhose, and complete seam with slip stitch, do not fasten off.

Ch 6, join with sl st to base of chain. Fasten off and weave in tail.

pan handlers

SIZE
About 4.5" (11.5 cm) long after felting.

YARN
Chunky weight (#5 Bulky).

Shown here: Stitch Nation Full o' Sheep (100% Peruvian wool, 155 yd [142 m]/3.5 oz [100 g]), in #2705 Peony (MC), #2260 Clementine (CC), 1 skein each.

HOOK
Size I-9 (5.5 mm) double-ended crochet hook.

NOTIONS
Large-eye blunt needle; laundry soap for felting.

GAUGE
Gauge is not critical to this project.

Keep hot pan handles safely covered with these colorful sleeves. Worked in Tunisian crochet and then felted, they're thick, soft, and super insulating. Never worry about cooking burns again!

DESIGNED BY KIM KOTARY

STITCH GUIDE

Tunisian Crochet

A row is worked in two steps, 1) the forward pass, which defines the stitch, and 2) the reverse pass, which is worked exactly the same for any stitch and completes the row.

To Work Tunisian Stitches in the Round

1st Half of Round:

ROW 1 (FORWARD PASS): With first yarn, pick up one-half the number of loops.

ROW 2 (RETURN PASS): Turn and slide work to other end of hook. With second yarn, work a standard Tunisian return pass.

2nd Half of Round:

ROW 3 (FORWARD PASS): Turn and slide work to other end of hook. With first yarn, pick up remaining loops of round.

ROW 4 (RETURN PASS): Turn and slide work to other end of hook. With second yarn, work a standard Tunisian return pass—one round completed.

Tss (Tunisian simple stitch)

Worked in the forward pass, insert hook from right to left behind the next vertical bar and yarn over, draw a loop through and leave on hook.

Tss2tog (Tunisian simple stitch two together)

Worked in the forward pass, insert hook between the vertical strands of two stitches, yarn over and draw through both stitches, leaving one loop to be worked off in the return row.

RetP (return pass)

Yarn over and pull through first loop on hook, *yarn over, and pull through 2 loops on hook; repeat from * across row.

Tss BO (Tss bind off)

With loop from last round worked, skip first vertical bar, *insert hook from right to left behind next vertical bar and yarn over, draw loop through both vertical bar and loop on the hook; rep from * until one vertical bar remains, fasten off.

Back Stitch

Insert threaded needle under two rows and up through layer of fabric. Count back one row and insert needle under next two rows. Continue this circular motion-ahead two rows from where the working yarn emerged from the previous row, and then back one row.

Tks (Tunisian knit stitch)

With yarn in back, insert hook from front to back between vertical loops and under horizontal strands, draw up loop from the back.

Note: These pieces are worked in continuous rounds; place a marker to identify the end of each round.

plaid handle

(forward pass = MC, return pass = CC)

With MC, ch 15, join with a sl st to form a ring (loop on hook counts as first stitch for Rnd 1).

RND 1

ROW 1 (FORWARD PASS): With MC, draw up loop in next 7 ch—8 loops.

ROW 2 AND ALL RETURN PASSES: Turn and slide work to other end of hook. With CC, work RetP.

ROW 3 (FORWARD PASS): Turn and slide work to other end of hook. With MC, draw up rem loops of rnd.

RND 2

ROW 1 (FORWARD PASS): With MC, Tss in next 7 ch—8 loops.

ROW 2 AND ALL RETURN PASSES: Turn and slide work to other end of hook. With CC, work RetP.

ROW 3 (FORWARD PASS): Turn and slide work to other end of hook. With MC, Tss in rem loops of rnd.

RNDS 3–15
Rep Rnd 2.

RND 16
ROW 1 (FORWARD PASS): With MC, [Tss2tog] 3 times—4 loops.

ROW 2 AND ALL RETURN PASSES: Turn and slide work to other end of hook. With CC, work RetP.

ROW 3 (FORWARD PASS): Turn and slide work to other end of hook. With MC, Tss2tog in rem loops of rnd.

With MC, Tss BO in rem 8 sts, fasten off, weave tail through front loop of sts to sew opening closed.

diagonal striped handle

Work as for Plaid Handle using MC for forward and return passes.

After completing handle, with CC, use backstitch to embroider diagonal stripes following chart.

wide striped handle

Note: Work as for Plaid Handle in completing rnd using colors and stitches as instructed.

With MC, ch 15, join with a sl st to form a ring.

RNDS 1–4: Tks in each st around; with CC, RetP.

RNDS 5–8: With CC, Tks in each st around; with MC, RetP.

RNDS 9–24: Rep Rnd 1–8 twice.

RND 25: With MC, Tss2tog around; RetP.

Tss BO in rem 8 sts, fasten off, weave tail through front loop of sts to sew opening closed.

FINISHING

Felting
Place handles in washing machine on normal cycle on hot water with 1 or 2 bath towels and some laundry soap. Dry until almost dry in a hot dryer with the towels. Place on pan handle to finish drying.

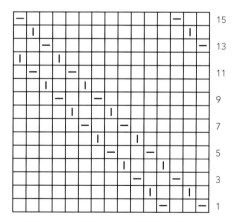

Diagonal Striped Handle

Embroidery Key

□ or Ⅰ = backstitch

berry pie

SIZE
8" (20.5 cm) in diameter.

YARN
Worsted weight (#4 Medium).

Shown here: Patons Canadiana Solid (100% acrylic, 205 yd [187 m/3.5 oz [100 g]), in #10010 Flax (MC), 2 skeins, and #10145 Dark Water Blue (CC), 1 skein.

HOOK
Sizes F/5 (3.5 mm) and G/6 (4 mm) or sizes to obtain gauge.

NOTIONS
Stitch marker; 6mm plastic eyes with safety backings; black acrylic craft felt, 1 sheet, 9" × 12" (23 × 30.5 cm); black embroidery floss; embroidery needle; fiberfill or stuffing of your choice; tapestry needle.

GAUGE
9½ sts × 10½ rows = 2" (5 cm) in sc stitch using larger hook. *Take time to check your gauge.*

This plush pie is too cute to eat! Display this confection on a pretty cake plate for a fun accent to your décor, or share it with a little one for the play kitchen.

DESIGNED BY ANA PAULA RIMOLI

STITCH GUIDE

Sc2tog
(single crochet two together)
Insert hook in next stitch, yarn over and pull up loop (2 loops on hook), insert hook in next stitch, yarn over and pull up loop (3 loops on hook), yarn over and draw through all 3 loops on hook.

pie

BOTTOM (WORKED IN SPIRAL)

With MC and larger hook, ch 2.

RND 1: 6 Sc in 2nd ch from hook, place marker to indicate beg of rnd, moving marker up each rnd.

RND 2: 2 Sc in every sc around—12 sc.

RND 3: [Sc in next sc, 2 sc in next sc] 6 times—18 sc.

RND 4: [Sc in next 2 sc, 2 sc in next sc] 6 times—24 sc.

RND 5: [Sc in next 3 sc, 2 sc in next sc] 6 times—30 sc.

RND 6: [Sc in next 4 sc, 2 sc in next sc] 6 times—36 sc.

RND 7: [Sc in next 5 sc, 2 sc in next sc] 6 times—42 sc.

RND 8: [Sc in next 6 sc, 2 sc in next sc] 6 times—48 sc.

RND 9: [Sc in next 7 sc, 2 sc in next sc] 6 times—54 sc.

RND 10: [Sc in next 8 sc, 2 sc in next sc] 6 times—60 sc.

RND 11: [Sc in next 9 sc, 2 sc in next sc] 6 times—66 sc.

RND 12: [Sc in next 10 sc, 2 sc in next sc] 6 times—72 sc.

RND 13: [Sc in next 11 sc, 2 sc in next sc] 6 times—78 sc.

RND 14: [Sc in next 12 sc, 2 sc in next sc] 6 times—84 sc.

RND 15: [Sc in next 13 sc, 2 sc in next sc] 6 times—90 sc.

RND 16: [Sc in next 14 sc, 2 sc in next sc] 6 times—96 sc.

RND 17: [Sc in next 15 sc, 2 sc in next sc] 6 times—102 sc.

RND 18: [Sc in next 16 sc, 2 sc in next sc] 6 times—108 sc.

RNDS 19 AND 20: Sc in each sc around.

RND 21: [Sc in next 17 sc, 2 sc in next sc] 6 times—114 sc.

RND 22: *Working through back loops only,* [sc 17, sc2tog] 6 times—108 sc.

RNDS 23-27: Sc in each sc around, join with sl st in beg sc of last rnd, fasten off, weave in ends.

TOP (WORKED IN SPIRAL)

With MC and larger hook, ch 2, place marker to indicate beg of rnd, moving marker up each rnd.

RND 1: 6 Sc in second ch from hook, place marker to indicate beg of rnd, moving marker up each rnd.

RNDS 2-12: Rep Rnds 2–12 of bottom—72 sc.

RNDS 13 AND 14: Sc in each sc around.

RNDS 15-18: Rep Rnds 13–16 of bottom—96 sc.

RNDS 19-21: Sc in each sc around.

RNDS 22 AND 23: Rep Rnds 17 and 18 of bottom—108 sc.

RND 24: Sc in each sc around.

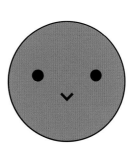

Berry Face

Top of Pie
Cut 5
(1½" × ¼")

RND 25: Sc in each sc around, join with sl st in beg sc, do not fasten off, do not turn.

EDGING

RND 26: (Ch 3, 2 dc) in same sp as joining, skip sc, sl st in next sc, *3 dc in next sc, skip sc, sl st in next sc; rep from * around, fasten off, weave in ends.

BLUEBERRIES

(Make 5.)

With CC and smaller hook, ch 2.

RND 1: 5 Sc in 2nd ch from hook, place marker to indicate beg of rnd, moving marker up each rnd.

RND 2: 2 Sc in every sc around—10 sc.

RND 3: [Sc in next sc, 2 sc in next sc] 5 times—15 sc.

RNDS 4–7: Sc in each sc around.

RND 8: [Sc in next sc, sc2tog] 5 times—10 sc.

Stuff with fiberfill.

RND 9: Sc2tog around—5 sc, fasten off leaving 6" (15 cm) tail for closing ball, weave in ends.

FINISHING

Blueberries

Attach 2 plastic eyes with safety backings and embroider floss between eyes with a V stitch for smile (see diagram).

Top

Cut 5 petal-shaped pieces from felt using template, and sew to top (see photo).

Assembly

Stuff bottom and align with top. Sew edges together right under the scallop edging (so the "crust" stays outside of the pie). Leave a slight opening. Sew 2 or 3 blueberries over opening (see photo). Sew remaining berries to the top.

berry pie

abbreviations

beg	begin; begins; beginning
bet	between
ch(s)	chain(s)
cl(s)	cluster(s)
cm	centimeter(s)
cont	continue(s); continuing
dc	double crochet
dec	decrease(s); decreasing; decreased
dtr	double treble (triple)
est	established
foll	follows; following
g	gram(s)
hdc	half double crochet
inc	increase(s); increasing; increased
lp(s)	loop(s)
MC	main color
m	marker; meter
mm	millimeter(s)
p	picot
patt	pattern(s)
pm	place marker
rem	remain(s); remaining

rep	repeat; repeating
rev sc	reverse single crochet
rnd(s)	round(s)
RS	right side
sc	single crochet
sl	slip
sl st	slip(ped) stitch
sp(s)	space(s)
st(s)	stitch(es)
tch	turning chain
tog	together
tr	treble crochet
tr tr	triple treble crochet
WS	wrong side
yd	yard(s)
yo	yarn over
*	repeat starting point
()	alternate measurements and/or instructions; work instructions within parentheses in place directed
[]	work bracketed instructions a specified number of times

abbreviations

techniques

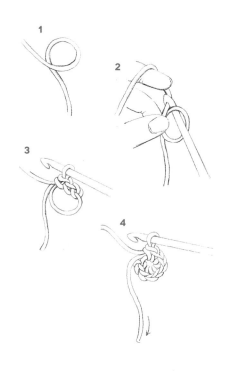

MAKING AN ADJUSTABLE RING

Make a large loop with the yarn **(FIGURE 1)**. Holding the loop with your fingers, insert hook into loop and pull working yarn through loop **(FIGURE 2)**. Yarn over hook, pull through loop on hook.

Continue to work indicated number of stitches into loop **(FIGURE 3**; shown in single crochet). Pull on yarn tail to close loop **(FIGURE 4)**.

CHAIN (ch)

Make a slipknot and place it on crochet hook. *Yarn over hook and draw through loop on hook. Repeat from * for the desired number of stitches.

DOUBLE CROCHET (dc)

*Yarn over hook, insert hook into a stitch, yarn over hook and draw up a loop (3 loops on hook; **FIGURE 1**), yarn over hook and draw it through 2 loops (**FIGURE 2**), yarn over hook and draw it through remaining 2 loops on hook (**FIGURE 3**). Repeat from *.

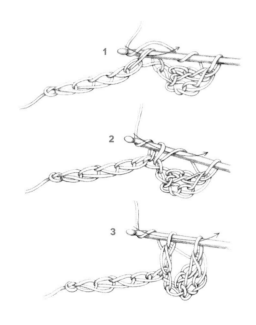

HALF DOUBLE CROCHET (hdc)

*Yarn over, insert hook in stitch (**FIGURE 1**), yarn over and pull up loop (3 loops on hook), yarn over (**FIGURE 2**) and draw through all loops on hook (**FIGURE 3**); repeat from *.

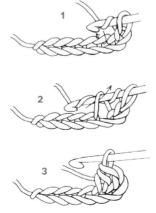

techniques

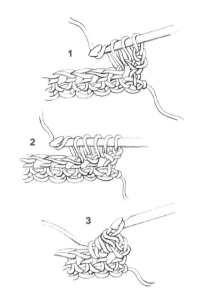

HALF DOUBLE CROCHET TWO TOGETHER (hdc2tog)

[Yarn over, insert hook in next stitch, yarn over and pull up loop] 2 times **(FIGURE 1)**, yarn over and draw through all loops on hook **(FIGURES 2 AND 3)**—one stitch decreased.

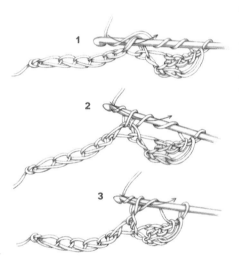

TREBLE CROCHET (tr)

*Wrap yarn around hook twice, insert hook into next indicated stitch, yarn over hook and draw up a loop (4 loops on hook; **FIGURE 1**), yarn over hook and draw it through 2 loops **(FIGURE 2)**, yarn over hook and draw it through the next 2 loops, yarn over hook and draw it through the remaining 2 loops on hook **(FIGURE 3)**. Repeat from *.

TWO SINGLE CROCHET INCREASE (2scinc)

Single crochet twice in the same single crochet stitch (increase).

TWO SINGLE CROCHET TOGETHER (2sctog)

Single crochet 2 stitches together (decrease).

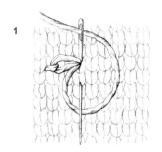

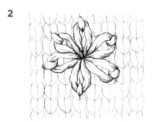

DAISY STITCH

Bring threaded needle out from back to front at center of fabric. *Form a short loop, and insert the needle right next to the spot where it first came out. Keeping loop under the needle, bring needle from back to front at the point where you would like the far end of the daisy petal to lie **(FIGURE 1)**. Pull loop snug and re-insert the needle on the other side of the thread to tack down the petal. Beginning each stitch at the same point on the fabric, repeat from * for desired number of petals **(FIGURE 2)**.

FRENCH KNOT

Bring threaded needle out of knitted background from back to front at the center of a knitted stitch. *Insert the needle into the upper right edge of the next stitch to the right, then out again at the center of the stitch below. Repeat from * as desired.

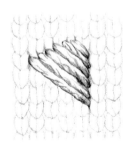

SATIN STITCH

This stitch is ideal for filling in open areas, such as the center of leaves or flowers. Work closely spaced straight stitches, in graduated lengths as desired, and entering and exiting in the center of or at the side of the crocheted stitches.

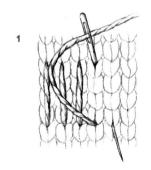

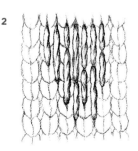

STRAIGHT STITCH EMBROIDERY

Straight stitches can be worked side by side or radiating out from a center point. For best results, avoid stitches that are too long, too loose, or too close together.

*Bring threaded needle out from back to front at the base of the knitted stitch(es) you want to cover. Insert the needle at the top of the stitch(es) you want to cover. Repeat from * **(FIGURE 1)**.

Work straight stitches, alternating long stitches with short stitches **(FIGURE 2)**.

techniques

resources

BERROCO INC.
1 Tupperware Dr., Ste. 4
North Smithfield, RI 02896
(401) 769-1212
berroco.com

BROWN SHEEP
brownsheep.com

CARON
320 Livingstone Ave. S.
Box 40
Listowel, ON
Canada N4W 3H3
(888) 368-8401
caron.com

CASCADE YARNS
cascadeyarns.com

LION BRAND YARN
135 Kero Rd.
Carlstadt, NJ 07072
(800) 258-YARN (9276)
lionbrand.com

PATONS
320 Livingstone Ave. S.
Box 40
Listowel, ON
Canada N4W 3H3
(888) 368-8401
patonsyarns.com

PEACHES AND CREME
320 Livingstone Ave. S.
Box 40
Listowel, ON
Canada N4W 3H3
(855) 418-1816
elmore-pisgah.com

PREMIER YARNS
2800 Hoover Rd.
Stevens Point, WI 54481
(888) 458-3588
premieryarns.com

QUINCE AND CO.
(877) 309-6762
quinceandco.com

RED HEART
PO Box 12229
Greenville, SC 29612-0229
(800) 648-1479
shopredheart.com

ROWAN YARNS
Green Lane Mill
Holmfirth
West Yorkshire
England HD9 2DX
knitrowan.com
Distributed in the U.S.
by Westminster Fibers

SPUD AND CHLOË
Blue Sky Alpacas
PO Box 88
Cedar, MN 55011
(888) 460-8862
spudandchloe.com

STITCH NATION
stitchnationyarn.com

TAHKI-STACY CHARLES INC.
70-60 83rd St., Bldg. #12
Glendale, NY 11385
(718) 326-4433
tahkistacycharles.com

WESTMINSTER FIBERS
165 Ledge St.
Nashua, NH 03060
(800) 445-9276
westminsterfibers.com

index

index

Add more inspirational Interweave titles to your crochet collection!

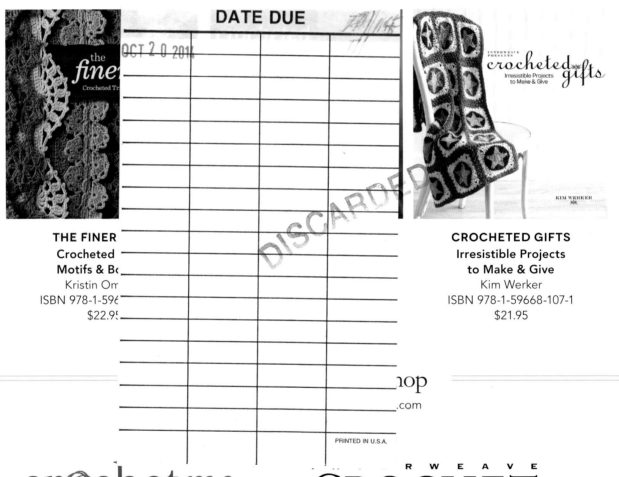

THE FINER
Crocheted
Motifs & B
Kristin Om
ISBN 978-1-596
$22.95

CROCHETED GIFTS
Irresistible Projects to Make & Give
Kim Werker
ISBN 978-1-59668-107-1
$21.95